ON BEING THE BOSS

Barbara McEwan, Edward Krauss,
and Forrest Gathercoal

CRISP PUBLICATIONS, INC.
Menlo Park, CA 94025

ON BEING THE BOSS

Barbara McEwan, Edward M. Krauss,
and Forrest Gathercoal

CREDITS
Managing Editor: **Kathleen Barcos**
Editor: **Andrea Reider**
Typesetting: **ExecuStaff**
Illlustrations: **Kurt Hanks**
Cover Design: **Kurt Hanks**

Copyright © 1995 by Crisp Publications, Inc.

Printed in the United States of America by Bawden Printing Company.

English language Crisp books are distributed worldwide. Our major international distributors include:

CANADA: Reid Publishing Ltd., Box 69559—109 Thomas St., Oakville, Ontario, Canada L6J 7R4. TEL: (905) 842-4428, FAX: (905) 842-9327

Raincoast Books Distribution Ltd., 112 East 3rd Avenue, Vancouver, British Columbia, Canada V5T 1C8. TEL: (604) 873-6581, FAX: (604) 874-2711

AUSTRALIA: Career Builders, P.O. Box 1051, Springwood, Brisbane, Queensland, Australia 4127. TEL: 841-1061, FAX: 841-1580

NEW ZEALAND: Career Builders, P.O. Box 571, Manurewa, Auckland, New Zealand. TEL: 266-5276, FAX: 266-4152

JAPAN: Phoenix Associates Co., Mizuho Bldg. 2-12-2, Kami Osaki, Shinagawa-Ku, Tokyo 141, Japan. TEL: 3-443-7231, FAX: 3-443-7640

Selected Crisp titles are also available in other languages. Contact International Rights Manager Suzanne Kelly at (415) 323-6100 for more information.

Library of Congress Card Catalog Number 94-68539
Edward, Krauss, Barbara McEwan, and Forrest Gathercoal
ISBN 1-56052-309-3

ACKNOWLEDGMENT
To Esther Kash for her help and support.

DEDICATIONS:
To our friends and families, we would like to express our deep gratitude for all your help, support, and understanding.

To Matthew, who in his own time has learned of the strength and magic in the written word.

To Evelyn Krauss, who in her life has been a teacher of lessons worth learning about perseverance, love, and loyalty.

ABOUT THE AUTHORS

Barbara McEwan, Ed.D. is a member of the Elementary Education faculty in the Professional Teacher Education program in the School of Education, College of Home Economics and Education at Oregon State University in Corvallis, Oregon. She is the editor of *Practicing Judicious Discipline*. Ms. McEwan's areas of research are classroom management and educational law. She has been an educator for 22 years.

Edward Krauss is Vice President, Manufacturing and Technology Development for the Greater Columbus Chamber of Commerce, Columbus, Ohio. His background includes 23 years of experience in personnel and training of government and private sector employees.

Forrest Gathercoal, J.D. is the author of *Judicious Discipline*, a model of law and ethics for the classroom, and *Judicious Leadership*, designed for Resident Hall personnel on college campuses. He is currently working on *Judicious Parenting*. Dr. Gathercoal has been teaching educational law for 20 years at Oregon State University in Corvallis, Oregon and serves as adjunct faculty to Lewis and Clark College in Portland, Oregon.

PREFACE

No matter how comfortable a work environment may be, it also has the stress that comes from spending time with others with whom you may or may not share some common interests other than that you have the same employer. Personal interactions may occur more frequently through electronic mail or written memos than in face-to-face conversation. Workplace environments are typically fast-paced, with high levels of stress where problems occur all at once, and everything needs an immediate solution. Depending on the level of worker loyalty, the perception of how urgent a situation is differs from one employee to another. You, the boss, are most important to this formula for organized chaos and job-related tensions.

You have probably spent time thinking about what kind of manager you want to be, or perhaps what kind of manager you don't want to be. Some managers believe the best way to achieve productivity is to take a fear and intimidation approach with employees and co-workers. The tension such managers are capable of generating ripples throughout the site. They seem to believe that their role is to be all things to all people: problem solver, counselor, judge and jury. They seem to be incapable of trusting those who work for them to act in responsible ways. They typically approach the decision-making process seeming to know what is best for all employees, what needs to be done and when it needs to be done.

Workers quickly get the message that their input is not welcome. The resulting discouragement often causes poor work attitudes and habits to develop. However, you may have a very different approach in mind. When you first moved up into the managerial position which you now occupy, you envisioned yourself being well-liked, while managing in the sort of cool, confident style you may have seen on some television show or in a job you held previously. You imagined yourself to be an open, caring manager who would empower workers by establishing a democratic work environment with shared decision making. "My door is always open," would be your motto. But once you were in the position, reality began to displace your daydreams.

As a manager you first had to learn to be constantly aware of the diverse interests in the workplace. Everyone has a personal agenda which may or may not coincide with the general welfare of the company. When attempting to build a democratic community in the workplace, you discovered that you were responsible for juggling upper-level management expectations, relations with the public, and the needs, ambitions, cultures and temperaments of the employees, while never losing sight of the bottom line. Despite your best intentions, you find yourself using fear and intimidation strategies, and justifying them by saying "Well, it works. When I act that way, the job gets done." The question we pose to you is "Toward what end do those strategies work?" What are you really accomplishing when you bully, shame and anger employees into a state of productivity? And finally, how long can your body and your spirit handle the daily stress of dealing with people who are learning to dislike and distrust you?

This book focuses on turning around those negative feelings by providing you with specific strategies for fulfilling the expectations of upper-level management, while facilitating a peaceful, calm and empowering workplace environment. We will present strategies for team building, effective communication, point out a red herring or two to avoid and include a discussion about ethics. Then we will place you in the middle of some real-world problems and challenge you to solve them. But, never fear, we're there with you. We will offer suggestions and ideas for solving the problems which include specific hints as well as some general notions for you to explore. These are problems that, as one manager recently put it, "explode in my inbox when I least expect it. As far as I know everything is fine and then, boom!" We will help you to anticipate coming explosions as well as manage the damage control when they do happen.

A democratic management style takes time and practice to fully implement, but higher levels of productivity appear to occur as an outgrowth of workers feeling valued and respected. Our ideas and your creativity will combine to assist you in creating and maintaining democratic, ethical and encouraging work environments. Throughout this book, we will set out some of the principles that can serve as a basis for creating this environment as well as provide a series of scenarios similar to the one which you are about to read in the Introduction. Scenarios will appear first with no explanations or solutions as an invitation for you to speculate on what might be your own approaches to the problems.

TABLE OF CONTENTS

INTRODUCTION

You are a manager in Moneycrunch.

After 9 years with Moneycrunch, Inc., you have risen to a middle management position. Moneycrunch is a firm providing financial analysis and investment services with seventeen thousand employees in 35 U. S. cities, plus offices in Canada, England, Germany and France. For some time there have been rumors in circulation about cutbacks and layoffs, and recently they have begun to hit. The downsizing is partly due to some top management decisions, and in fact the CEO was recently fired. Additional problems are not the fault of anyone within the company, but rather the result of a long, slow recession coupled with significant changes in the way the world's economic institutions work.

Seven months ago, after a series of long, painful meetings and planning sessions, you were forced to cut your staff from 60 to 45. At the same time, the company is aggressively seeking new clients, researching and developing new financial services and products and paying extra attention to those clients who have stayed with the firm. Thus, although the staff has shrunk significantly, the work has not. In fact, in some areas it has increased. Now, seven months after the big layoff, you observe the following about your staff:

1. Morale couldn't be worse. Everyone is hunkered down, concentrating on their work. No one shares ideas or information. No one pitches in and helps anymore. As a result,

1

an office that once worked well as a great team effort has become 45 isolated workstations. In the past, people picked up phones for their co-workers when needed. They offered each other advice and freely shared it. They formed informal teams and pooled information and skills in a cooperative atmosphere. All this has almost disappeared.

2. Most people are upset because they think that more work from their fallen comrades has come to their desks than to others. There is a reluctance to complain, but you know this feeling is widely, perhaps universally, shared.

3. People are afraid that they will be laid off next. Some are already looking for other employment, cutting into their concentration and commitment to Moneycrunch. Although as a manager you know that no further cutbacks are planned at this time, you are not sure how to make them feel more secure. You are afraid that you may lose some valuable people to new jobs at a time when you can least afford it.

People are afraid they will be laid off next.

You know that the company's financial situation has stablized. In fact, it is starting to turn upward, although new hires to ease the workload will not be brought onboard for several more months, and then very slowly. It could be two years before your staff is up to sixty people again. Until such hiring does occur, how can you persuade your staff that the worst is over? How do you begin restoring and rebuilding the team spirit that is almost gone? How do you get people to accept the new, heavier workload, which appears to be long-term, possibly permanent? How do you convince them that the workload is shared as fairly as possible? How can you be most effective in this difficult situation? Top management is watching!

At the very end of this book we will ask you to solve by yourself the Moneycrunch, Inc. scenario. We will offer only a little input. Because you might be tempted to flip to the end of the book right now, here is a peek at the concepts that form the premise for this book. As with most of the managers you will meet in these pages, the manager described above is pretty much convinced that all the problems in the workplace have to be solved in a top-down fashion. In other words, this manager thinks of himself as the "fix-it" person. The series of questions that appear at the very end of the scenario indicate that this person is attempting single-handedly to cure all the difficulties the workers are experiencing. Remember, when it is your turn to wrestle with these situations, that you are surrounded by individuals who do all of these jobs everyday and know them well. Too often that rich source of information is ignored when it comes to problem solving. If asked, workers could provide solutions to any of the issues your company is facing, because they deal with the situations on a daily basis. But their potential input is often overlooked as employers rush around trying to solve all of the problems themselves.

This book is designed to help you reduce the stress you may be placing on yourself because you want to fix everything, for everyone, right now. Your own frustration and sense of being overwhelmed, the angry behaviors you might engage in as evidence of your emotional state and the message you send the workers when you refuse to allow them to help with problem solving only transfers more pressure from them to you.

THE NEED TO WORK TOGETHER

It is not unusual for the working hours to exceed the waking hours we spend with our loved ones. As a result, at work we are forced to become very much like a substitute family, needing each other to cooperate in order to accomplish tasks. We share eating spaces and bathroom facilities, and pursue financial security together. A key element of success or failure in all of this is the relationship between you and each individual employee.

The hiring of an employee is simply a trade.

The hiring of an employee is a trade. The emloyee gives time, energy, brain power, muscle power, dedication and loyalty. The employer gives promise to pay for the immediate time worked and an implied promise of long-term, continued employment.

The question then becomes, is that all there is to the trade? Probably not. If companies are to grow and prosper, it would seem that they have to do more. Angry and frustrated people will create dysfunction in the workplace that could lead to bad attitudes, abuse or quitting. A manager who has not given time and thought to developing a personal approach to leadership that will avoid or

Drawing on the United States Constitution, huh?!

defuse such problems may end up experiencing high levels of employee dissatisfaction. In such situations, managers who have not mapped out their administrative strategies will tend to blame their problems on their workers. In the end they may fire disgruntled employees, and in worst case scenarios, face lawsuits.

Company personnel, like family members, would like to stay together and share happy, productive lives. But that goal is only possible if there is a standard of consideration, sharing and civility that is consistently maintained. Experience tells us that any effort put out by workers who have been treated disrespectfully will be accompanied by silent anger, passive submission or covert efforts to derail success.

When and if such employees quit, they take their skills with them. Companies that experience a high turnover of employees lose knowledge and experience. Worse, the companies lose the value of a mutual and long-term commitment. Smoothly run organizations want every member of the corporate family to succeed personally, while sharing their efforts to achieve the common goals of success for the company. As manager, you will find that civility in your workplace leads to the establishment of trust and mutual respect among you and your employees.

THE FUNDAMENTALS

This book integrates concepts to build a solid managerial position which are drawn from two principal sources. One source is the United States Constitution, which forms the framework for laws that govern our society. The other is the ethical position taken by management. It is our belief that the areas of constitutional law and ethics can be combined to provide a unified direction for decision making that will lead to cooperative, democratic work environments.

BUILDING A FRAMEWORK FOR MANAGEMENT DECISIONS

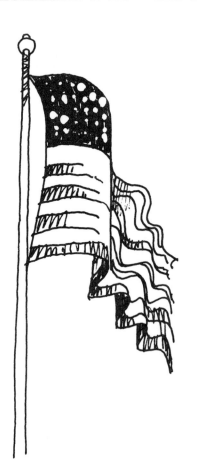

*The Constitution as
a framework for
management decisions*

In order to achieve your vision of being a democratic manager, it is wise to examine the United States Constitution. This book will provide some basic legal concepts which are designed to serve as a guide as you sort through the scenarios we present. It will also be useful as you set about applying these concepts to your worksite. Once we have discussed the basics of the constitutional principles that will serve as a framework for this book, we will add some fundamental ethical guidelines.

Being a judicious manager means accepting and practicing two basic tenets. First, all employees will be respected and treated in accordance with the rights they are guaranteed in our society. Private employers might reasonably create rules that deny certain individual freedoms, such as insisting that First Amendment rights to expression will be secondary to having employees wear some form of uniform. Nevertheless, the respect and dignity that is inherent in our constitutional freedoms can be used to enhance all interpersonal relations, including those occurring in the workplace.

Second, ethical considerations will be used to maintain and enhance the democratic workplace environment. The difference between an ethical workplace structure and one lacking in ethics would be the difference between a manager who criticizes an employee in front of co-workers and an employer who creates an opportunity to engage in a private problem-solving session with a difficult employee.

We all live under a form of constitutional government which gives certain freedoms to the individual, while at the same time protecting the needs of the majority. Individual rights are not guaranteed, but neither are they easily denied by the majority.

While we all learn to understand the concept of majority rules, seldom are we taught very much about the other side of the balance. People often know little about their constitutional rights or, more often, have misinformation about their constitutional rights. Many citizens do not understand that our system of government carefully considers the rights of individuals along with the needs of the majority when making decisions that affect the way we live. Our constitutional form of democracy tries to create a level playing field through sharing mutual respect and responsibilities. It is this same language of civility that we will be applying to the workplace in order to help managers maintain democratic environments.

THE BILL OF RIGHTS

American constitutional liberties spring from the first ten amendments to the Constitution, better known as the Bill of Rights.

Constitutional rights exist to protect three basic values: **freedom, justice and equality.** The legitimacy of the American legal system stems mainly from these fundamental values. However, controversy in our society at large and workplaces in particular exists over the question of when, how and if it is possible to limit individual freedoms.

Freedom is a most cherished value in our country. A democratic manager must determine when one worker's actions or words need to be limited so as not to disrupt everyone else's right to work in a safe, protected and productive work environment.

Justice is concerned with due process and deals with basic governmental fairness. In the workplace, due process becomes the center of all the issues that swirl around hiring, firing and plans of assistance. When democratic managers take steps to correct problems of behavior and attitude, due process should define the when, where and how of the corrective response.

Equality presents us with the problem of distributing burdens and benefits. The proposition of all people being created equal has never meant that we all possess the same abilities, interest or talents. The aptitude for leadership surfaces quickly and should be encouraged. Basing promotions on a standard of ability helps managers avoid accusations of bias as to who moves up and who does not.

The three values of **freedom, justice** and **equality** are reflected in the United States Constitution and are basic to understanding individual liberties and civil rights contained within the framework of the United States government. If managers wish to establish and maintain democratic working environments, it only makes sense to model the structure after the framework already in place in our larger society.

FIRST AMENDMENT

Congress shall make no law respecting an establishment of religion or prohibiting the free exercise thereof, or abridging the freedom of speech or of the press; or of the people to assemble, and to petition the government for a redress of grievances.

It is most important to begin with the understanding that this amendment is vital to the fabric of our lives in the United States. It allows us to be who we are and to express ourselves in all the many and varied ways we might choose to do. First Amendment protections of free speech and expression play themselves out in the workplace in many ways. Expression includes the clothing, jewelry, buttons and other adornments worn by employees as well as posters, pictures or slogans displayed around workstations. An employer may wish to limit the dress of workers by insisting that they present a consistent image to the public. But if there is no such policy, an employer might create an uncomfortable set of circumstances by arbitrarily banning some forms of expression while endorsing others. For instance, an employer might decide that women wearing slacks to work creates too casual an image, while the same manner of dress for men is not only acceptable but expected.

Managers can avoid such contradictions by creating policies that are consistent and free from bias. In other words, setting a standard by modeling appropriate dress and encouraging workers to present a professional image to the public. Modeling creates a clear message of expectations, and empowers workers to use their good sense about what is and what is not okay to wear. When an individual needs more clarification, a private conference will usually take care of the problem.

FOURTH AMENDMENT

> The right of the people to be secure in their persons, houses, papers, and effects, against unreasonable searches and seizures, shall not be violated, and no warrants shall issue, but upon probable cause, supported by oath or affirmation, and particularly describing the place to be searched, and the persons or things to be seized.

Although protection from illegal search and seizure does not extend to one employee accidentally stumbling upon contraband in a second employee's locker or desk, citizens in any setting have an expectancy of privacy. Demonstrating respect for workstations and lockers by requesting that workers retrieve equipment or materials for you rather than obtaining them yourself is a sound managerial practice that builds a sense of trust with workers.

FOURTEENTH AMENDMENT

All persons born or naturalized in the United States, and subject to the jurisdiction thereof, are citizens of the United States and of the State wherein they reside. No State shall make or enforce any law which shall abridge the privileges or immunities of citizens of the United States, nor shall any State deprive any person of life, liberty, or property, without due process of law, nor deny to any person within its jurisdiction the equal protection of the laws.

The last two clauses of the Fourteenth Amendment have had the most significant impact on our personal and professional lives. The first of these, known as the due process clause, provides the legal process by which employers can counsel or, if necessary, fire an employee. The latter clause, known as the equal protection clause, serves as the constitutional foundation for all our laws and rules prohibiting discriminatory practices. This clause is broadly interpreted in cases dealing with all forms of discrimination, including sex, race, national origin, the handicapped, marital status, age and religion. Because due process and equal protection are such vitally important concepts to the rest of this book, we wish to offer further clarification.

DUE PROCESS

. . . nor shall any State deprive any person of life, liberty or property, without due process of law . . .

Picture the blindfolded figure of justice standing strong and confident as she adorns the thresholds of our country's court-houses, her outstretched arm holding the familiar scales. Imagine one scale brimming with all the employees in your workplace actively engaged in their jobs. On the other side of the scale, picture one lone worker, gazing apprehensively at the group of people amassed on the other side. This graphic illustration symbolizes the essence of due process.

In its simplest terms, due process is a legal effort designed to balance individual rights with the need to protect the interests of society. The court's scale of justice will tip to protect the needs of the group only when the state is able to show a compelling reason, such as health and safety, as to why public interest should outweigh individual constitutional rights. Conversely, if the government cannot demonstrate a compelling state interest, then the rights of

Due process is designed to balance the individual's rights against the interests of the larger organization (society).

a single individual will weigh more heavily than all those who crowd the other side of the scale. As the scales of justice tip in favor of one person, all the other workers must learn to practice respect and show consideration for that individual's rights.

In order to fully understand the implications of the due process clause, we must examine the last phrase with particular care.

". . . of life, liberty, or property" defines those rights which may be deprived through due process by governmental action. It is interesting to note that the framers of our Constitution used just three words to protect our past, present, future and even death at the hands of the government.

The word life refers to the loss of life at the hands of the government—the execution of a criminal. Stated in positive terms, the government may deprive a person of life, liberty or property only if the individual is given due process.

The second word, liberty, begins with the present and includes all our future acquisitions and aspirations. All the jobs we will hold, the ranks to which we will be promoted and the salaries we will earn are included in the concept of liberty.

Property covers such tangible properties as real estate, personal property, money and contracts of employment, as well as intangibles like eligibility and entitlement to welfare payments. For this reason, it is a much easier concept to grasp than the notion of future belongings and opportunities that are associated with liberty. Employers who are concerned about the success of their employees demonstrate in their words and actions that they understand and value the workers' right to both property and liberty guarantees. Managers who strive to protect the present realities and future opportunities of their workers often enjoy a special relationship in the workplace. Employees who know their managers are concerned about the property issues of here and now, and aware of implications revolving around liberty interests that represent secure futures, will respond with loyalty and support.

Substantive due process pertains to legislation, the rule or the law itself, and means a basic fairness in the decisions that are made. The rule should: 1) Have some rational need for its adoption; 2) Be as good in meeting the need as any alternative that reasonable people would have developed; and 3) Be supported by relevant and substantial evidence.

In other words, substantive due process implies that our nation's laws and decisions must be legal before our government can deprive someone of life, liberty or property. As managers create rules, they must consider whether a rule will have a negative effect on the interests of each employee. For example, a manager who ties pay increases and promotions to an inconsistent set of standards, would be jeopardizing the concerns of all workers. Whether they are being rewarded or punished, the arbitrary nature of the environment in which they are working will effectively obstruct their ability to be successful.

Sometimes managers will carefully think through rules, making every effort to ensure fairness, and still have an employee challenge the regulations. Keep in mind that whenever someone questions a rule or seeks clarification of a decision, that individual is legally exercising Fourteenth Amendment substantive due process rights.

Procedural due process in our society relates to the decision-making process used when determining whether a rule or law has been violated. In the workplace, it is the process that defines how a worker is dismissed. Basic fairness is required and has been interpreted by the courts to include the following: 1) Adequate notice; 2) A fair and impartial hearing; and 3) The right to appeal the decision.

Adequate notice includes such procedures as documented charges, evidence to be used against an employee, a reasonable amount of time to prepare a defense, the time and place of the hearing and adequacy of form (oral and written). A fair and impartial hearing includes elements such as a meaningful opportunity to be heard, state a position and present witnesses. It also may include the right to counsel, presentation and cross-examination of witnesses, and reviewing written reports in advance of the hearing.

With few exceptions, the due process clause allows all administrative interpretations, decisions and rules to be appealed through public structures established for that purpose. The decision or rule may be appealed to a higher state or federal administrative agency and then referred to an appropriate court.

THE OTHER HALF OF THE BALANCE

It is important to understand when, where, how and why rights can be denied. The scales of justice represent individual freedoms, but also group responsibility, and in our society one person has the right to act on, believe in and demonstrate personal values as long as those actions and demonstrations don't result in disruption for everyone else. Most of us understand that our rights may be limited to protect others from what might be inappropriate forms of expression. For instance, telling an individual not to yell "fire" in a crowded theater is the most common example of when a First Amendment right is limited to protect the safety and welfare of all others.

An individual's expression or actions can be restrained when there is a compelling state interest for doing so. For the purposes of this book, the compelling state interests have been condensed to four: Property Loss and Damage, Legitimate Workplace Purpose, Health and Safety, and a Serious Disruption of the Workplace Environment.

PROPERTY LOSS AND DAMAGE

Care of property is usually an easy concept for most of us to understand and few would argue that they have a right to damage equipment or other parts of their workstations. Adequate training, when appropriate, must be provided in order to reduce the risk of property damage occurring as a result of ignorance. Property also refers to personal items brought in by employees. While it is impossible to completely prevent theft, it is important to recognize management's responsibility to provide employees with a safe means to protect their possessions. Lockers, locking desks or file cabinets with locks are all useful to protect personal items. Notices should be posted stating that theft is possible, and workers are encouraged to take responsibility for making sure their property and that of the plant is secure.

LEGITIMATE WORKPLACE PURPOSE

Generally speaking, all policies and decisions that have a legitimate employer motive would come under this heading. Decisions about uniforms, assignment of tasks, promotion policies and other employer concerns for the smooth management of the workplace can all be justified according to this compelling state interest. The key is the word "reasonable." The administrative structure cannot arbitrarily establish its rules and procedures. For instance, young, attractive female employees cannot be assigned to the front desk while older women and males are assigned to offices. Using physical characteristics, as opposed to ability, when determining job responsibilities or workstation assignments is discriminatory. While a manager may claim the reason for making such decisions lies in presenting a youthful, attractive image to the public, such assignments cannot be justified under compelling state interest. On the other hand, managers can insist on a professional standard of dress for all front desk employees that sets a business-like tone throughout the workplace.

HEALTH AND SAFETY

This compelling state interest typically commands more attention than the others. The issues surrounding liability should be commonly understood by managers so that prudent steps will be taken to prevent accidents. Beyond the issue of liability is the more ethical issue of trust in the workplace. When workers believe that management has not taken sufficient measures to protect their well-being, productivity is diminished by serious dissatisfaction.

The government has established clear guidelines for work-place safety and we will not review those regulations in this book. Our primary concern will be with the mental health and well-being of workers and the overall tone of the work-place environment.

SERIOUS DISRUPTION OF THE WORKPLACE ENVIRONMENT

While employers may personally view any number of behaviors exhibited by employees as disruptive, the key to understanding this compelling state interest is the word "serious." That is, in what actions might an employee engage that would cause productivity to come to a halt. There is a distinction between behaviors an employee might exhibit that would make a manager uncomfortable and what behavior is truly disruptive to the smooth function-ing of the workplace. We offer the following three very important questions that should be reviewed before a rea-sonable, democratic decision can be rendered. Unless all three questions are weighed carefully, poor judgment will likely follow.

1. *What is serious?*
   Each situation must be decided on its own merits and may vary from one place to another. For instance, shouting across workstations in a machine shop might be considered a standard method of communication for a noisy environment, but in a front office the same shouting would be inappropriate as well as seriously disruptive.

2. *Must the serious disruption have already occurred, or is the threat of a serious disruption enough to sustain the rule or decision?*
   Often rules and decisions are based on the fear that some-thing may occur, although the incident has never hap-pened or is not likely to happen. Typically, employers need to be able to show a pattern of disruption occurring as a result of certain behaviors in order to create rules banning an action. But many managers operate under the "This Might Happen" theory of rule making. They will restrict the actions, dress and speech of employees because they fear repercussions that exist only within their suppositions.

However, there is a balance to be maintained around this issue. The "This Might Happen" rationale will support a rule which affects health and safety. Employees do not need to get their hair tangled in equipment in order to create a policy which states that long hair needs to be tied back when working around machinery. On the other hand, a rule banning long hair from the front office because it might offend customers has more to do with speculation than reason.

When managers can show employees that injury or other problems have resulted in the past because of specific actions, rules banning future similar displays will make sense and usually receive compliance.

3. *For whom should the rule be intended, the individual who is exercising constitutional rights or the majority who are bothered by the individual's exercise of those rights?*
When it comes to slogans or symbolic representations on pins, buttons, T-shirts, posters or other forms of First Amendment expression, managers are frequently called upon to take some action against an individual whose statement is offensive to others. In the scenarios that will follow, this question for determining what is a serious disruption will surface again and again. As you will see, there is no standard resolution. If an employee does not like the fact that the next workstation is occupied by a male with shoulder-length hair, tolerance becomes more the issue than an employer telling a productive worker to cut his hair. On the other hand, a proliferation of posters displaying nude women in suggestive poses, while perhaps common in some workplace settings, might be detrimental to the productivity of female workers. In such cases, the balance would tip in favor of removing the posters in order to protect the success and workplace stability of the women present.

As you move toward a more democratic management style, there are a few other issues with which you will be faced. For instance, when you imagine yourself as the perfect democratic manager, you might imagine a scene where everyone comes together to vote on all major governance concerns. But before doing so, we need to explore the pitfalls involved in such a strategy.

THE MAJORITY MAY RULE BUT IT DOESN'T ALWAYS VOTE

Looking at business situations when the individual's rights are at conflict with the needs of the majority.

Managers often believe they are creating a democratic environment when they ask for a consensus from the group or allow employees to vote on an issue. This does not always accurately reflect democratic principles and can easily injure a feeling of community when a close vote on an issue divides the organization. For example, workers may wish to vote that abortion literature should not be posted on a bulletin board in the lounge area that has traditionally been used for a variety of notices. Telling an employee that abortion information may not be posted involves an arbitrary limit on First Amendment rights and, therefore, even though the decision to permit only certain types of information in the lounge may have come about by a majority vote, it is not necessarily a decision that can be supported legally. Our democratic form of government only allows us to vote on those issues which are not protected by the Constitution.

This book analyzes a number of situations that bring an individual's rights into conflict with the needs of the majority. Let's begin with an example to clarify why we should not allow the majority to vote on individual rights. Imagine that you have an employee who is burning incense at her workstation during breaks. The incense has a strong odor and lingers in the air long after it has been put out. Adding to the problem is the rule that workstations have been designated "No Smoking" areas.

The worker who is burning the incense insists that she is within her rights because by burning incense she is engaging in religious expression, and is exercising her First Amendment rights. However, there are others working near her who are equally entitled to a work environment that will not distract them. It might seem sensible and fair at first to ask the workers to vote on whether or not this employee should be allowed to burn incense. But when we examine this situation more closely, a vote on this issue would result in one of two outcomes; either the worker would be summarily deprived of her First Amendment right to religious expression, or other workers would compromise their healthy and comfortable environment.

The situation instead should balance the needs and interests of both sides. A small committee of employees should be appointed to look into possible times for religious expression. This might include burning incense at an appropriate place located inside or outside of the building, or a manner in which religious expression could be carried out without infringing on the needs of others. In this case, manner might be defined as the way incense could be burned and the scent confined to the worker's station. These same guidelines could be applied to a variety of workplace concerns, such as smoking.

On other occasions, voting on issues would be an appropriate way to settle things and should be encouraged. For example, there is no problem with employees deciding, within reason, when break times should occur or which park will be used for the company picnic. But on matters affecting the rights of workers, managers should help to develop and employ the administration of reasonable time, place and manner.

COMMUNICATING CONCERN, VERBALIZING SUPPORT

While the law provides a reasonable framework for decision making, it will not answer all the questions or solve all the problems that managers face today. Accordingly, we are also stressing the importance of employing effective communication strategies when working toward solutions. You will find certain terms in the scenarios that might need some clarification. With that in mind, we are providing you with a few definitions of terms and some accompanying examples.

Site-Management Team: This is one of many descriptors for a group of employees empowered both by their employers and fellow workers to assist in the decision-making processes of companies. Managers bring problems to the group and, with some input into the discussion, abide by the group's decision or take the group's recommendations back to the employees for a decision. When managers are trying to unravel some complicated work-related difficulties, a site-management team can often present ideas that would never have occurred to just one person. There is strength in numbers and often creative solutions to be found as well. While it is not an easy process to put in place, it can be a very powerful communication tool between employees and employers.

I-Messages: Taken from the writings of Thomas Gordon, the "I-Message" is an approach to expressing concerns when talking with personnel. In a non-I-Message exchange, a manager who is dealing with a difficult employee might say "You're coming in late on a regular basis and that has to stop." The I-Message shifts the focus of the comment away from the employee in order to reflect your concerns about the issue of late arrivals, as opposed to the character of the worker. An I-Message appropriate to the situation might be, "I am concerned about the fact that you've been late a few times recently. I have noticed that the others in your department seem upset by your late arrivals." A statement like this avoids a defensive response from the employee because you are merely stating what has been observed. I-Messages can serve as an opening to a dialogue about how the situation will be corrected.

I-Messages are also useful when you feel angry. Taking the time to phrase an I-Message is often the equivalent of counting to ten. When pushed to the wall, having to think of a way to express feelings through an I-Message prevents the first words that are flying into your mind from being the first words you speak. This strategy can save you from serious embarrassment and the need for endless apologies.

Power Struggles: As it appears in this text, a power struggle is recognized not only through the behavior of the person who is struggling, but also in the reaction of the person being struggled against. Rudolf Dreikurs describes a power struggle as a conflict that represents one person trying to seize control over a situation by openly challenging the person who is in charge. The person being challenged identifies the power struggle, in part, because he or she feels threatened by the attitude or verbal assault.

The best response to a power struggle is to back out as quickly and gracefully as possible.

The best response to a power struggle is to back out as quickly and gracefully as possible.

Allow for "cool-down time." You are not backing down or avoiding the issue, but rather you are creating an opportunity for both you and your employees to process what has happened before meeting privately in a one-on-one situation. If your attempts to speak with the worker are met with anger and hostility, try responding with something such as "It seems like you're having a tough day. Do you want to talk about this now or would another time be better for you?" With a little practice, managers can learn to look past the offensive language and focus on the larger issues of maintaining a comfortable work environment for everyone.

Nothing positive can ever be gained by exerting your power over an employee. A recently observed minor power struggle between a supervisor and an employee ended quickly but not without serious consequences. The supervisor ended an encounter over the allocation of time to some task by saying "Well, I guess your decision depends on how much you want to keep your job." While the manager had exerted power to bring the situation to an end, the look of anger and embarrassment in the eyes of the employee indicated that the working relationship between them had been seriously damaged. If the manager had instead waited for a time to meet with the employee privately, and used that time to negotiate a compromise, the scenario might have had a very different outcome.

CONFLICT RESOLUTION

Using this phrase is a very workable communication strategy.

As it is being currently defined, conflict resolution refers to verbal communication techniques that focus on keeping the conversation separate from personalities. What follows are some specific techniques for reducing stress and mediating conflicts in ways that will sustain a pleasant and supportive climate in the workplace.

COMMUNICATION STRATEGIES

Avoid road blocks: According to Thomas Gordon the biggest roadblock is "I told you so." Whoever you are speaking with will know you told them so. No positive outcomes will result from saying it to a worker.

Use clarifying statements: Another very workable idea is using the phrase "What I hear you saying is . . ." when you are trying to clarify something another person has said. "What I hear you saying is that you are having trouble working with the person whose desk is next to yours." If that is in fact what you were told, employees will often go on to provide you with more information that will ultimately help you to help them resolve the problem. If you have misunderstood, your error will be clarified. Either way, repeating back what you heard, prefaced with "What I hear you saying is . . ." will give you more data than you would otherwise have.

Establish a comfort zone: When meeting one-on-one with employees, try to create an environment of equity. You do not need to establish your authority by sitting behind a desk. Your authority is already understood. After all, it's your office. It is wise to have a work area in your office, a round table or some other way of sitting together with another person other than on opposite sides of a desk. A chair at the side of the desk is not the same thing as a work area where you share equal space. If there is another place in your facility that allows for a confidential meeting, you might consider using it. That will move you both onto neutral turf and help to break down any real or imagined barriers to an open, honest conversation.

Greet the employee warmly. Whatever went on before this meeting, whatever the level of hostility, you can afford to be gracious. Begin with something like "Come in. I guess we have something we need to talk about."

Develop the question: When working through a problem, the first requirement is to get more information. Angry, sullen behavior is only the manifestation of whatever is wrong. Responding to the outer symptoms while ignoring the causes will never help you to resolve the conflict in a manner that is satisfactory to either of you. You can get information by asking questions as opposed to lecturing.

If you have employees who are coming to work late, or missing work, what you need to know in order to help fix the problem is "why." Too often the worker will have no clear idea why the problem is occurring or will initially be unwilling to share the information. Patience is required. Begin with a question like "What's happening?" I understand that the proposal you're working on is behind deadline. I'm wondering if you can tell me what's happening with that?"

Thomas Gordon refers to such questions as "door openers." Beginning the discussion with a door opener such as "It looks as though you are really upset," provides the employee with an opportunity to give you information. The employee can choose whether or not to take advantage of the opportunity. Your tone should be conversational and reflect genuine curiosity. The less judgmental you have made the workplace environment, the more likely the employee will be to seize upon the door opener in order to discuss a grievance. Door openers such as this help to get conversations going and let the other person know you are tuned in to their feelings.

It is important to remember that the person you are talking to probably knows the rules and is aware of the mistake that's been made. By asking leading questions and listening carefully, underlying issues begin to emerge. In addition, questions allow you to take a more thoughtful approach with employees and allows them to retain the dignity as they respond to questions rather than accusations.

Avoid the word "but:" As in, "I think you did a great job on this paste-up, but . . . if you had only . . ." The problem with this sort of phrasing is that the "great job" has been seriously diminished in its impact and the employee is left waiting for the next shoe to drop. Words of encouragement and praise should not be the steppingstones to criticism. Another approach might be "This paste-up looks great. I really like the illustrations you included. I am wondering if the centering on the address is dead on. Would you please check it to be sure?" In this message, the compliment stands alone and the concern is specifically addressed.

Conflict resolution is a practiced art. The techniques cited here will help to get a manager started. Combining these ideas with the ethical concepts that follow will help a manager resolve most issues in a calm, reasonable and judicious manner.

Many people experience momentary panic when faced with some of the scenes mentioned above. Their overriding concerns seem to be that the "right thing" will come out of their mouths when they are faced with a critical situation. Our advice is to relax. It is your attitude and mindset that will save the day, not a question or phrase that you have memorized in the hope that it will fit whatever crisis might come along. If you are focused on the success of your employees and on the maintenance of a calm and supportive workplace environment, the particular words are not as important as your demeanor when dealing with a problem. You may not have a perfect question or response ready when you most need it, but just listening for awhile is very effective. Good communication often lies not in the words we use, but in the spaces between the words. When your whole management style is centered on mutual achievement, no matter what words you actually use, those around you will hear a clear message of encouragement.

ETHICAL CONCEPTS

This section on ethics is designed to give managers some basic "dos," ideas that always seem to effectively support the mental well-being of employees, as well as some "nevers" to avoid. If you can avoid saying and doing things that are certain to result in negative feelings, while trying to remember a few basic strategies for sustaining positive feelings, it becomes easier to be creative when reaching for ideas that will help to end problems with everyone's dignity intact. When you stay away from the nevers and try to incorporate those ideas that should always be part of your managerial style, you can feel comfortable knowing that your actions will not lead to anxiety or anger, but rather will be part of a consistent, supportive relationship with employees.

THE DOs

Always model responsible personal and professional behavior.

When interacting with employees, remember that the model of behavior you are setting speaks a thousand times louder than any words you will ever use. Be aware of the impression you are making at all times. Save temper tantrums and complaints for private times away from the workplace.

If you want workers to maintain orderly workstations, avoid lecturing about the value of neatness when your own desk is piled high with file folders, loose papers, and unanswered memos. Hypocrisy and insincerity undermine integrity and have a negative effect on developing personal and professional relationships.

Always develop fair, reasonable rules and expectations for the workplace.

Management by whim can result in workers feeling embarrassed, alienated and uncooperative. If you are a manager who makes it up as you go along, you can depend on a lot of job dissatisfaction among your workers, if not lawsuits charging you with discriminatory practices.

Always focus efforts on trust, motivation, encouragement and building a positive work environment.

Statements such as "I knew you'd have this in late" have no place when trying to build confidence and productivity. Such comments hurt and are often mulled over for hours in the mind of the employee who was singled out. Whatever the circumstances, a judicious manager needs to consider the long-term effects of an inappropriate or unguarded comment.

When someone does a good job, let that person know the effort was appreciated. Listen when someone comes to you with an idea. If it has merit, take the idea to the site-management team. Be conscientious about making sure the team knows from whom the idea came. If there are problems with the idea, tell the employee the basic notion is good but you have some concerns. State your concerns and give the employee an opportunity to correct the problems. Let your employees know every day through your words and actions that they are valued members of your team.

Always enjoy administration and be proud that you are successful in your profession.

Have confidence that your interpersonal skills and abilities will make a difference in the attitudes and efforts of your employees. A positive and professional attitude is invaluable when dealing with management problems.

THE NEVERs

While there are ideas and attitudes we should always try to remember, there are also responses we should work diligently to avoid—the "nevers."

Never demean an employee, especially in the presence of other workers.

Sarcasm meant to be clever or a "good chewing out" might appear at first glance to be an effective method of handling an errant employee. But experience teaches that these approaches only destroy relationships. Once destroyed, they can never fully be regained. When a problem does happen, find the time to hold a private conversation.

Invite the employee to a quiet corner or into your office. Offer coffee, tea or a soft drink. If your manner is calm and matter-of-fact, the employee is far less likely to become defensive and the odds of a positive outcome are greatly increased.

Never compare employees.

"Why aren't you as good as _____ at this job?" is never helpful. Workers want and deserve to be judged on their own merits and not be thrust into the shadow of others.

Praise can create an equally difficult set of headaches in a work environment. Reserved parking spaces for the worker of the month or other public rewards can often isolate an employee from other workers. When we hold up one employee as a shining star, that person can find coming to work a lonely experience. As stated earlier, an employee should always be complimented for effort. Offering the compliment privately can make the exchange that much more meaningful. It is always pleasant when the worker has the option of whether or not to share your words with anyone else.

Never demand respect, earn it.

Respect, like love, implies feelings which cannot be taken, only given to others who merit it. As a manager seeking to earn respect, first you must learn to give respect. If you are unsure of ways to demonstrate respect for your workers, begin by putting yourself in their shoes. If you would want input into decision making, structure ways for them to have that experience. If you would feel distrust because someone was going through personnel files and indiscriminately sharing the information with others, refrain from doing such things yourself.

Never be dishonest with employees.

Never be dishonest with employees.

An employer who is open and authentic earns the trust and respect that is necessary for a positive work environment.

Whenever changes occur, whether they are something as major as the schedule, something as minor as the paint on the wall or something in between, be honest and inform your employees about the possibilities. Managers will often decide on major changes without consulting any employees, shifting workstations, moving offices, and leaving employees wondering why they weren't consulted.

Refrain from making serious changes in the office structure without getting broad input into how things might be improved. Do not think that what is said or done behind the closed door of a head office will stay there. A basic truth of any work environment is that it is characterized by a well-functioning, truly impressive grapevine. Words exchanged confidentially will quickly find their way to the rest of the plant. Nothing destroys productivity faster than rumors of change that seem, on the surface, to be scary and threatening. Respond to rumors in a proactive way by keeping your workers well-informed and a genuine part of any decision-making process.

Never accuse workers of not trying nor ask them to try harder. Help them try again or suggest another way to accomplish the task.

Employers must communicate a message of faith in the workers' ability to change as well as offer support through the process. Remember that you are dealing with adult learners who may have experienced frustration when trying to master a new concept or skill in the past. Telling a worker who is having difficulty mastering some task that he or she should try harder is the same as constructing a wall of concrete in his or her path.

How can people possibly learn anything useful from the phrase "try harder?" They already have tried as hard as they possibly can to accomplish the task. Now is the time to offer some different approaches. Be prepared to provide on-site training, one-on-one assistance or whatever it takes to help your workers succeed.

Never get into power struggles with workers.

Sometimes power struggles are difficult to avoid, but with common sense and patience managers can become experts at averting them. If you sense a power play is developing with an employee, back off. These are no-win situations and should be handled privately, through individual discussions and mutual agreements.

Although this sounds easy, it is not. When your ego is on the line, an employee is in your face and everyone is watching, backing down may be the furthest thing from your mind. The fear is that you will lose control if employees see you respond in such a way. Actually you will be perceived as a person of grace and dignity, and worthy of respect.

Resolving conflicts peacefully and privately establishes an excellent model for your employees. Your ability to encourage them to do the same will be enhanced when you demonstrate that nothing is lost by removing yourself from the struggle so that you might settle the problem later, away from the general staff.

We have discussed power struggles both in the section on communication skills and in this section on ethics. They will also appear in the scenarios that follow. This is not accidental. Power struggles are difficult experiences and often emotionally wrenching. It is important to understand them and learn to acknowledge the role you can play in avoiding them. Your energies and talents can be used far more productively elsewhere.

Never become defensive.

Do not let your pride get out of hand and diminish your personal and professional qualities in the eyes of your employees. If you created the problem, be prepared to apologize. If you have made an error, acknowledge it and sincerely ask for forgiveness. As a result, you will very likely be considered an upfront person with human frailties and will suffer no loss of dignity.

Never lose control of your feelings.

Remarks made during the height of emotional upset can cause both frustration on the employee's part and regret on yours. Take a deep breath, be silent for a moment and calmly formulate an I-Message that is devoid of emotional

Never lose control of your feelings.

overtones. Remember that your working life takes place in a fishbowl located under a microscope.

Never underestimate the importance of professional style and demeanor.

Maintaining a professional attitude and appearance in the workplace defuses many potential problems that might otherwise occur. Your dress, your choice of words and the jokes you tell all have a serious impact on the workplace. Remember that your personality and demeanor ripple out to the farthest corner of your facility.

"Bedside manner" in every profession is very important, and the way things are phrased to workers as well as what is said can often be the difference between an uncomfortable situation getting worse and a rough spot that is quickly smoothed over. As with any of the "nevers" we have listed, it takes practice to develop a style that others will try to emulate. You can do it. Keep in mind when you are less than your best that perfect practice makes perfect. Don't give up. When you blow it, apologize and start again.

Never think that being consistent means treating all workers alike.

Having consistency in the workplace means identifying individual differences among employees and providing the assistance that will enable each one to be successful. The compliment from you that is treasured by one employee may be offensive to another. Look at issues from diverse perspectives before taking action. To always respond to problems in ways that reflect your own upbringing and culture may mean that you are failing to successfully reach all employees. Take the time required to know your employees, and learn to appreciate and manage their individual differences.

BEGINNING AT THE BEGINNING

Build a framework for your rules and decisions.

When you first became a manager what pieces of information about yourself, your philosophy and your approach to problems did you impart to the people now working for you? It is essential to begin by building a framework for your rules and decisions. While your mode of operation will certainly reflect your personal values, stating them early and clearly will help employees to understand how things will be run in their shop. Being proactive in sharing your strategies through conversations and training sessions will help to ensure that democratic techniques will be practiced throughout the worksite.

Managers considering the use of various democratic techniques for working with staff members are sometimes consumed by the "what ifs," such as "What if I treat one employee one way and another employee another way?" The fear of being perceived as inconsistent or weak can cause some employers to apply consequences across the board for problems that arise whether it makes sense to do so or not.

A judicious manager must keep in mind that employees bring with them to the workplace a variety of personal needs and concerns. While the ideal situation might be described as a company of workers who all leave their private lives at the door, the reality is that tensions and worries are constantly being mulled over while employees are otherwise "on task." Because these private matters are so varied, they must be dealt with in creative and individualized ways.

A community of workers who mutually support each other's efforts and strive for a congenial atmosphere are often responding to deliberate efforts on the part of a manager to create trust, respect and cooperation from the first moment he or she stepped into this role. While it might not be necessary to provide lengthy explanations of your management style, it is critical to spend some amount of time with employees constructing a foundation for all the decisions that are to come. Let employees know who you are, what you believe and that you are there to support them in order for you to all succeed together.

APPLYING THE CONCEPTS

In the following scenarios, there are many issues that surface concerning the legal and ethical aspects of personnel management. First, you will have an opportunity to read the scenario in its entirety. Make notes in the margin as to how you would respond to the developing situation. Then, you can read the scenario again. This time it is annotated with your notes to help you understand how a democratic manager would employ all the concepts we have discussed to resolve the problems presented.

OF BUTTONS, TOLERANCE, AND KEEPING THE PEACE

You are the personnel director of a large, old factory in a major industrial town. Your workforce, almost two thousand employees, is roughly divided evenly among Caucasians, African-Americans and Hispanics. The work is difficult and can be quite dangerous unless people pay careful attention to their machines and processes.

He showed up at work wearing a "White Power" button.

One day a Caucasian employee shows up wearing a White Power button attached to his work shirt. Immediately there are angry reactions, although no one walks off the job or starts fighting. However, it is clear to all of the management staff that the potential for serious trouble is real. The anger being felt by two-thirds of the employees could cause inattention that would lead to industrial accidents in addition to the potential for serious conflicts among the workers. Comments made to crewleaders and other floor supervisors have been to the effect that if the employee does not remove the button, it will be removed for him.

Later that afternoon there is a regularly scheduled site management team meeting, and the button is the first order of business. Lots of opinions are spoken, some at the same time. "Just tell him he can't wear it." "He has a con-

stitutional right to wear it." "That's right! Free speech!" "Wait a minute, isn't this like shouting fire in a theater?" "No! This is his belief." "No, that can't be right. What if people believed in the Nazis. Could they wear swastikas in here?" "We just wouldn't let them." "Why not?" "How could we stop them?" "Why don't we just ban all symbols. That would be fair. Right?" "Well, I don't know about that. My secretary wears a cross every single day. That's a symbol, isn't it?" "Okay, just good symbols." "What does a good symbol mean?" "What if he wants to wear a button that just says WP instead of White Power? What do we do then?"

At this point they all slow down, remember that they have a personnel manager and turn to you for advice. What do you say?

Believe it or not, there is a lot of good news here. This is exciting stuff! These people are wrestling with the same issues that have engaged the greatest legal minds in our country's history. The short answer is "No one ever said tolerance is easy." It is the most difficult concept we deal with in our country as we seek to protect those who burn flags, practice their religion by engaging in the ritual sacrifice of animals or wear white robes to a cross burning. The good news is that your employees are thinking and talking about some very serious issues dealing with our basic freedoms; they are discussing topics that rarely see the light of day outside of a civics class. Don't be afraid to let them air their views and discuss ways in which conflicting beliefs can be subordinated to maintaining a productive, safe work environment.

What you need to ask yourself first is "What are the issues?" As you prioritize the list of issues, realize that the predominantly important issue is safety. That has to be your foremost concern. This is an example of the balance at work. There is a First Amendment side to this story, but health and safety must come first.

But as we examine the balance further, it is equally important to realize that a safe environment ultimately is the responsibility of each worker. Hazardous conditions are no more caused by a White Power button than they would be if the plant employed several racists and an African-American came to work wearing a button with the image of Martin Luther King on it. All sorts of personal distractions, both physical and psychological, can present potential hazards on any given day and workers must be trained or receive training in ways to handle stress and maintain their faculties at all times.

To further explore the issue of the button, let's examine the conversation occurring at the site management team meeting.

"Just tell him he can't wear it."

While this would resolve the immediate concerns of those offended by the button, it is the solution to nothing. The worker whose button has been banned will be angry and might well find other, even more destructive ways to express his views. Again, any slogan on any button could be offensive to anyone. Unless you do not have a better use for the time you spend at work, you might not want to assume the responsibility for gauging the potential irritation quotient of one particular button or another.

"He has a constitutional right to wear it."

That's right. He does. Particularly if your plant has had no stated policy against wearing such symbols up to now. Again, this is where tolerance becomes difficult. It is easy to be tolerant of ideas or life styles that are different but nonetheless compatible to our personal world views. The problem is that many people also believe it is somehow equally okay to be intolerant of those ideas we find truly offensive. Our Constitution, however, is designed to protect all of us as we exercise our rights, as long as we are not directly harming anyone else.

Help your site team to explore ways of encouraging tolerance in your worksite. One idea is to designate a bulletin board as a free speech area where any and all views can be shared. One button in a plant can draw a great deal of attention. On the other hand, a bulletin board that displays a wide range of ideas reflects the jumble we all experience in the real world. No one item becomes any more important than any other. Such a bulletin board might well eliminate the need for buttons; it will certainly lessen their impact. But let's return to the discussion.

"No, that can't be right. What if someone believed in the Nazis. Could they wear swastikas in here?"

The answer to that question is yes. Just as the American Nazi Party could march through Skokie, Illinois, so can the swastika or the White Power button be worn in this factory. These are, after all, only symbols.

"Why don't we just ban all symbols. That would be fair. Right?"

Actually that would be a rule based on "this might happen." There is no pattern of health and safety problems or of serious disruption in this factory based on the wearing of one button or another, so a manager would probably find it difficult to justify such a rule. Unless a manager can demonstrate incontrovertible proof that this or that button is directly linked to accidents or violence in the plant, buttons should be allowed. An individual has the right to wear a symbol of his or her beliefs and co-workers have the right to develop their levels of tolerance.

So as personnel manager what do you do? Well, begin by thanking them for engaging in a very interesting discussion. Express your concern for their physical and mental well-being and let them know that their health and safety is of prime importance to all the management of the factory. Schedule some brown bag discussions about topics of tolerance and understanding. Invite various groups to bring in speakers if they would like. Encourage workers to engage in an open dialogue about their beliefs with the understanding that differing views will be listened to, argued with but not fought about.

If you have not provided staff training on problem solving and conflict resolution, now would be an excellent time to do so. Let them know the motive for the training is to enhance the safety of the plant. Encourage them to practice the strategies they have been taught, and model their practice at every opportunity.

As for the worker who is wearing the button, there is no need to address the issue with him one way or another. The staff development and brown bag lunch program are designed to enhance the workplace environment for

Ralph is given to playing the grandfather or the great uncle role.

everyone. There is no need to single this person out as the "cause" for changes that will help everyone. If he does say anything to you about it, you might thank him sincerely for providing you with an opportunity to openly discuss issues that should have been brought forward long ago.

RALPH, MONA AND THE BALANCE

You are the manager of an accounting and data processing department in a division of a Fortune 200 company. You have seventeen employees. One of your employees is Ralph. He has been with the company thirty-seven years, and will be retiring in less than three years. Although he was educated and hired long before the days of computers and electronic spreadsheets, he has learned enough of the new techniques to remain an acceptable employee. Whatever accounting weaknesses he has are certainly offset by his great depth of knowledge of the company and its customers. His recall of early corporate history has come in handy in more than one research project. You look forward to his retirement, because you would like to hire someone with much stronger computer skills. But for now, he is just fine winding down his career.

Ralph is given to playing the grandfather or great-uncle role and since several of your employees are over twenty years younger than Ralph, they like having him around to talk with on lunch breaks. Both men and women regard him as a comfortable listener, an elder statesman of human relations to consult about dating, marriage, divorce, retirement plans or how to buy a used car. Lunch is always characterized by one or two people huddled with Ralph over their trays in the cafeteria.

Ralph often calls men "son," and women "dear" or "honey." No one else in the department uses such terms. In fact it is discouraged throughout the company in personnel policy manuals and the occasional memo. However, Ralph has always seemed to be exempt. He is not demeaning or condescending when he says it, it is just part of his persona. There has never been a formal objection to his use of these terms.

You recently had an opening in your department, and posted it as required. A woman named Mona applied from the sales division. When you checked with her supervisor, you were told that she is "an excellent worker with strong skills, but that she is occasionally irritable." This is described to you as the result of a recent bitter divorce that has left her in a difficult financial situation.

Within a few weeks of hiring Mona you have found that both comments were understatements. She is fast, accurate, dedicated and has already made two suggestions that will improve the audit trail on accounts payable without increasing the paperwork. In short, she is a real find.

Mona is also the owner of a short fuse. She had a few tense words on two occasions with two separate employees in the first ten days. They were not major problems, and there were no really angry words, but you sense that Mona could become an irritant in your shop.

Before you decide just how to handle this, Mona asks to see you. She says that Ralph calls her and other women "Honey," and that she objects on two grounds: she is offended by the familiarity and it violates company policy.

You answer that she is certainly correct, but that Ralph has been around so long, and that it has been his style for so *long, that no one really has noticed until now. You suggest that she is hearing these words with, as it were, new ears.*

Sensing an opportunity, you promise to discuss the situation with Ralph. Then, you talk about the two incidents in the past weeks. Mona agrees with you that she could have been more polite, and says that she is under a lot of stress, but will try to remember what you said and to act accordingly.

When you call in Ralph the next day, you tell him that his use of endearments is not proper in the office setting (sounding a bit stuffy as you listen to yourself) and that he should try to stop using them.

Ralph says, "Mona complained."

You look at him and say, "Well, yes, but that isn't the point. Look, I have been negligent not to have mentioned this a long time ago. We are talking about company policy." Ralph agrees to try to change his ways and you part on a friendly basis.

A few days later, you are standing in your office door, talking to your secretary, when the following occurs. Mona is walking around a corner of a desk carrying a stack of papers. Ralph is walking towards her, but turns his head to answer a question from across the room. Naturally, they collide. Papers everywhere. Ralph takes her arm for a moment, says "Sorry, honey" in his automatic way, and stoops to pick up the papers. Mona looks down at him and shouts, "Don't touch me! And stop calling me honey!"

The whole room is silent. Everyone looks at them, and then at you. What do you do?

The scenario presented here is filled with a compendium of subtle and not so subtle legal and ethical issues. First of all, the Fourteenth Amendment guarantees of substantive due process and equal protection are working in Ralph's favor as an older employee. Even though his skills may not match the skills of younger personnel, who have received more specific training in computers, he has an expectation to his property interest in his job, his liberty interest in his retirement fund and the guarantees that capricious rules designed to discriminate against age will not be used as a means of forcing him out before he is ready to retire.

The concern lies with Ralph's unconscious use of terms that could be misunderstood. While there has never been a formal objection, there may very well be tension created by the use of the terms. Even though Ralph is well liked, the phrases he is choosing to use have been frowned on as part of company policy. The concern here is that the manager is allowing a pattern of interaction to occur simply because Ralph is old. That the manager is making exceptions to the rules simply because of Ralph's age can only be described as arbitrary and capricious decision making. While "son" or "honey" may not be red flags, nevertheless, the manager in this situation is establishing tacit approval of terminology not supported by the company and is doing so only because of one individual set of circumstances. To make such exemptions is to take a step away from legal consistencies as well as an ethical posture of support for all workers.

Referring to Mona's personal history, workers bring their troubles into the workplace. The question a democratic manager must answer is, will the behavior of the employee who is dealing with a personal problem create a serious disruption to a comfortable working atmosphere? In this case it is equally important to ascertain if Mona's "irritable" behaviors are being tolerated or even ignored because she is a woman. This is another form of discrimination. An employer who is protecting Mona's liberty or future interests would be wiser to recommend counseling or other positive avenues for change, rather than possibly damaging Mona's opportunities for upward mobility by passing along such information.

Mona's privacy rights would make sharing information about her personality possible on a "need to know" basis. If the problem is so serious that it is affecting her performance, then it would make sense for her manager to create some form of intervention for her. If it is not, why pass the information along? In this scenario Mona will begin working in a new setting with at least one strike against her.

Any professional who keeps records on other individuals, such as students, employees or clients must also be aware that in order to protect liberty interests, records should not contain subjective information, and be specific about stating exactly what the problem is. "Mona is irritable" could mean that she does not join in on coffee breaks, that she periodically slams her fist on the desk, that she forgot to say "Good Morning" to her manager last week or that she is known to periodically hit people over the head with her briefcase. When passing along information on any employee, managers are on much safer ground legally if they stick to specifics and refrain from using terms that are vague and potentially damaging.

It must be obvious that this manager's belief in the "benign neglect" approach to problems is going to blow up. Mona should be called in as soon as the first incident occurs. Begin by congratulating her on the improvements she has brought to your division. Let her know she is an appreciated member of your team. Using an I-Message, gently introduce the fact that you have become aware of a problem that occurred recently and ask if there is something with which she might need some help.

Tell her if she needs to "vent," your door is always open.

If and when a second incident occurs, express to her your continued support and disappointment that she did not come to you with the latest problem. If she is truly a valued member of your team, your swift intervention at the first sign of trouble will be viewed as a show of support and should help to solidify her support of you.

This manager's style eventually begins to turn sour. By sitting back and watching potential problems develop rather than using early intervention strategies, the scene is set for outright conflict. Workers in this division have been given the message that problems will not be dealt with by management and therefore they will seek resolution to situations by themselves. Because territory and ego will inevitably be involved, it is almost a certainty that the resolutions will further fracture working relationships rather than heal the wounds.

But it is not too late to rectify the situation. Begin with a sincere apology to Mona for allowing a violation of company policy to go unchecked. You have been caught with your company codes down and responding in a defensive manner will only act to further aggravate the problem. Let Mona know you will work to correct the situation.

Schedule a meeting with her and Ralph. You should serve as the facilitator at this session. Your goal is to establish an opportunity for conflict resolution. Begin, again, with an apology for not effectively carrying out company policy and let Ralph know Mona's concerns. Work together with both of them to resolve the conflict.

The issue is not what has happened but what will happen. Ask each of them to suggest ways that they can work together comfortably in the future. Let Mona know that you strongly support and value both of them. With this said, encourage both of them to brainstorm how each will handle the next incident. Thank them for their time and help with the situation. Unfortunately, that is not what this manager chooses to do.

The manager's response is at least unfortunate and most certainly biased. The manager has chosen to respond by "blaming the victim." Because her "ears are new" she is responsible for feeling offended. Mona does not need to hear the equivalent of "There, there." The manager is clearly wrong in this situation and should be comfortable enough with himself or herself to acknowledge the error.

The issue of ethics is important here. Individuals who are in managerial positions too often respond defensively when they are caught doing something inappropriate. If managers cannot get past their ego involvement to correct a problem they have allowed to fester, the situation will only grow worse. A manager who is secure enough to admit an error commands a great deal of respect and loyalty. Managers who protect their egos by placing blame everywhere but on themselves typically inspire contempt and distrust.

After having spoken with the manager, Mona has learned a more subtle lesson. "Don't go to the manager with problems, you will only get in trouble yourself." This last paragraph underscores why this manager should have talked to Mona immediately after the first incident. Mona now has the message that if there is a problem she had better handle it herself. If she is in a financial bind, she may fear for her job if she goes to the manager again. Because she has demonstrated a deficit in the area of interpersonal skills, it is a safe bet that when she does try to resolve the conflict herself, she will probably do so in an inappropriate fashion.

After speaking with Ralph, this manager makes a common mistake made by parents, teachers and so many others placed in positions of power. Rather than working with Ralph to develop strategies that will help him to remember to use other words, this employer simply says "Cut it out." By not providing Ralph with alternative ideas, there is very little hope that this brief conversation will result in an alteration of lifelong behavior patterns.

This is how mismanaged conflicts inevitably erupt. Had early interventions occurred, this situation would most likely not have happened. However, it is never too late to change things and all is not lost. The manager should move to the situation and quietly make sure both are all right. They are both embarrassed and nothing positive will come out of embarrassing them further. Therefore, although you might want to meet with them, now is not the time. Help to pick up the papers, make sure they are both feeling more at ease and without directing it at either of them, see if you can interject a little humor into the situation.

Later, approach each of them privately and request a meeting. The format for this session should be similar to the conflict resolution meeting described earlier. Again, use the time to plan strategies for alternative behaviors should something like this occur in the future.

The bigger problem here is that the conflict erupted in public. After meeting privately with Mona and Ralph, schedule a staff meeting within a few days. Without making any personal references, discuss in general the issue of conflict resolution. You have allowed certain situations to continue without acting on them. Get input from all members of your site management team and **act on it, act on it quickly, act on it publicly.**

It must be clear at this point that a legal, ethical approach to management works best when used as a preventive strategy. If the person in charge spends his or her time putting out fires, the time is ill-spent. Preventive strategies of problem solving, counseling, protecting confidentiality and modeling respect for employees will go a long way toward building an atmosphere of equanimity and dignity.

TROY'S DISARRAY

Your company, Frajit, Widget and Steambuckle, has been growing rapidly as a sales service organization. This has caused a rapid hiring spurt and the present facility is seriously overcrowded. Desks are placed face-to-face, cubicles have been subdivided into smaller cubicles and aisles have narrowed. The company is in the process of completing construction financing for a new office building, but it will be somewhere between 18 and 24 months before everyone will be able to move into the new offices.

Among your most valuable employees is Troy, an accounts manager. He has the ability to handle a vast number of phone calls and information requests. Unfortunately, although the office has excellent computers, much of the work still requires a great deal of reading, verifying and writing on numerous NCR forms and looking things up in various vendors' manuals and catalogs.

Troy's desk and surrounding area are always in a mess. He has stacks of catalogs and manuals surrounding him, papers stacked up on his desk and a few stacks on the floor around his desk. As manager you figure that part of his problem might be the volume of work he handles, which is more than almost anyone else. Part of the problem is a shortage of sufficient support staff, who cannot be hired until the new building is completed, and part of it could be reluctance on Troy's part to take a break now and then to file, stack and throw away.

Your concern is not with the esthetics of the situation, since you know that there is no direct relationship between a neat desk and a productive employee. Your concern is for the safety of Troy and his co-workers. With many people hurrying back and forth in the narrow aisles, often carrying books and files, the trip points that now surround his desk have become hazards for the staff. No one has been hurt yet, but it certainly seems like an accident waiting to happen. In addition, you

Troy's desk and surrounding area are always a mess.

have recently noticed others letting their areas get cluttered, and the catalogs stacked on the floor are creating more trip points all the time. People seem to be following Troy's example and there is a feeling that because this is a temporary set-up there is not a great investment on the part of the workers to keep this office looking good. After all, newer and more spacious offices are coming.

But those new offices are more than a year away, and the accident potential around Troy's desk is high and the problem is spreading rapidly. What do you do?

This is a classic example of "Oh gosh, I should have seen this one coming." With space that is not expanding while the personnel roster is, a wise manager should be looking down the road at how to make the cramped, although temporary, conditions tolerable as well as safe for everyone. But even though that wasn't done, it's not too late to salvage the situation. The primary concern to be addressed has to be OSHA regulations and the common welfare of all the workers in this department. But while the safety issue is a great concern, and it should be, you need to figure out a way to get the mess taken care of without embarrassing a good, productive employee. Troy may need some organizational skills, some new desk equipment or an attitude adjustment. As the democratic manager you are working to become, it is very important to explore all the possibilities, figure out why the problem is occurring and then to take steps that will resolve the problem and leave Troy's spirit intact.

So let's begin with the easiest solution. This office needs some stackable bins, desk top book cases, trays or any other item you can order in mass amounts out of a catalog of office equipment. Whatever the cost, it's cheaper than the liability suit that would accompany a worker injured by tripping over a stack of catalogs on the floor. And whatever equipment you do order can easily be put to use in your new location.

You should not be the one to determine how much of what gets ordered. You could handle this solution in one of two ways. No matter which plan you decide to use, you should first share OSHA regulations with everyone. A posted notice would probably be a good beginning. Post the notice on the same day that you begin to take action on the problem. That way the notice is shared information and not something that could come off looking like parental nagging. After all, this is government regulation stuff, not your rules.

You might meet with your site team and have them select those items that they agree would provide a temporary solution to the problem until the move is made. Suggest that they select and share with everyone four or five items from which workers can choose, depending on individually determined needs, so if one worker wants desktop bins and another a new file cabinet, both options are available. They should also announce a ballpark figure allotted to spend. Another approach would be to just make the catalogs available to everyone along with the ballpark figure and a deadline for handing in requests posted next to the OSHA regulations. The issue is that the problem must be resolved, all the workers are responsible for the safety of each other and the equipment can be transferred over to the new setting. Then all you have to do is hope that Troy, along with everyone else, puts the new equipment to the use for which it was designed.

But let's suppose that the items arrive, get unpacked and everyone cleans up their act, except Troy. It's a safe bet then that one of two things might be going on. Troy may lack organizational skills. You may want to provide some staff training for everyone in this area and justify the time spent under health and safety considerations. Find a trainer who can work with your staff to help them manage with more people in less space. Even though this is a temporary situation, the skills are nevertheless valuable and will give you some specific items to work on with Troy.

If, after the training, the problem still isn't cleaned up, you can meet with Troy and say something like "Remember that suggestion the trainer made about organizing files. I'm just wondering if you think that could work for you? I want to work this situation out, Troy. The area around your desk just isn't safe for you or any of us." You need to make it clear that you must remain firm on the safety issue. You're on Troy's side and you want to help. He needs to meet you half way in this collaborative effort to solve a potentially dangerous situation.

If the mess remains, you should consider whether or not you might be dealing with another, deeper problem. Troy could be sending you a message that he is not happy about some situation, and now it becomes your job to figure out exactly what the true nature of that message might be. He may be trying to tell you that he is aware of how heavy a workload he has and how it compares to that of his co-workers. It may not be a source of personal satisfaction to him that he can do almost double the work of those around him. He may be using his messy work area to say "It isn't fair for me to always be the one to pick up everyone else's slack." Whether or not that is the case, if it is his perception of the truth and he is unhappy about it, you need to try to empathize with his point of view.

It's time for a more direct approach and an opportunity to use some of the communication skills we discussed earlier. Given your current physical layout, a private moment at Troy's desk may be an impossibility. If so, ask for a brief conversation in your office. Begin the discussion with a friendly I-Message. "I am wondering how those trays and things everyone ordered are working for you." You need to be direct but sincerely interested. He will certainly know why you're asking and you will no doubt get one of two responses. The first will be something like "I know. I need to clean up my space. I am just so busy." Ask him if it's possible to arrange for someone to help him with a few tasks while he gets the area organized. Again, your goal here is to help and to support him, not to be a parent figure nagging about a messy bedroom. If, instead, he responds with an angry "Get off my case," try using a question to get the conversation started. "Troy, I get the feeling there is more going on here than some difficulty with your workstation. I'm wondering if I can be of help to you?" He may or may not open up about whatever the underlying problem is, and that's okay. You have demonstrated concern and respect. If he chooses to disclose information, talk through whatever problem he surfaces and forget about the desk for the time being. At the end of your conversation say something like "I'm glad we talked. I'm sort of in a box here, Troy. I've got to keep this place as safe as possible even though the space is tight. I'm glad to support you in any way I can. I need your help with this whole thing. Can we work on it together?" With most employees, under most circumstances, you will get the change desired. If Troy continues to resist, you may need to begin the process of removing a valued member of the team. The scenario about the "Internal Assassin" should provide some guidelines for you if that becomes necessary.

TAXING TIMES

For the last three years you have been the manager of the Special Tax Services Department of the Redink Investment Trust Co. You have seven employees on your staff, all with at least three years of service in the department, plus some who transferred in after additional years in other departments. As a result, the team is quite efficient and knowledgeable about the tax reporting duties of the department. Year-end closing is a difficult and stressful period. The company's fiscal year is October 1, and no one on your staff is permitted to take vacation from August 15 through October 15.

Sue, one of your most competent employees, has always been very successful at juggling her responsibilities at work and as a single parent of an eleven-year-old son who suffers from diabetes. On Sunday night, August 20, Sue had to rush him to the hospital because his sugar levels were extraordinarily high. She did not come to work on Monday. Since then

Your team had become quite efficient and knowledgeable and Sue was an important part of it.

her son has been home a few days, and back in the hospital for several more. Sue has been in the office only for part of some days, and has been on the phone to her son's doctors and to the hospital during some of that time.

It is now early September. Sue's attendance and attention continue to be erratic. You feel that you have an impossible-to-solve management problem.* You have a good, dependable employee with a child who has what is now a life-threatening illness. Although it seems to you that Sue could put more trust in the medical staff, you realize that you have never walked in her shoes and you find it hard to suggest that Sue worry less about her child and pay more attention to her job. However, year-end is approaching and the team is not functioning as it should. The rest of the staff is upset but feels guilty about being upset with Sue because of her problems.

You must get the tax work done accurately and on time. There is no time to train a temporary replacement. Either Sue needs to focus more on her job, or the others need to pick up more of the load when they are already doing as much as they can. What can you say and do?

You can start by moving past the tinge of gender discrimination that is at the edges of this scenario. This is not about a single woman who is the parent of a sick child, it is about everyone of us who is trying to juggle work and home responsibilities in ways that will allow us to pay equal attention to both. It is also about anyone of us suddenly stricken by a personal catastrophe. And that is where you must begin. A medical emergency is something that could happen to anyone of the workers in that office. Pull back from your desire to lecture Sue about the decisions she is making and take a long hard look at the decisions you have made that contribute to the problems you are encountering.

It does not require a crystal ball to know that whatever can go wrong, probably will go wrong. If you have a "crunch time" when no one is permitted even a vacation,

---

*For an excellent book on this topic, order *Work and Personal Life: A Manager's Perspective* using the information in the back of this book.

it is inevitable that a personal problem will occur in the life of one of the workers. In fact, you might consider yourself lucky to have gone three years without such a situation. A little advance thought given to a Plan B might have helped to alleviate your current stress and Sue's agony over where her time should be spent. But it's never too late to establish contingencies and now is as good a time as any.

Begin by meeting with Sue privately. Let her know she has your unqualified support. You understand that her situation could be the situation of any of you and that the issue you are now facing together is how to help her through this difficult time and still not drop the ball at work. Ask her permission to bring the issue of creating a contingency plan to an open meeting of the group. Assure her that this meeting will not be about her, but about helping the team strategize various ways they can fill in when necessary.

At the meeting, the first step you should take is to make your intentions clear that the discussion is not to be about Sue, but about the general welfare of the team. Do not equivocate on this issue. If someone mentions Sue's name, interrupt long enough to refocus on the larger issues at stake.

Once the ground rules have been established for this meeting, get creative. If a member of the team is forced to be absent during this time, and there is not enough staff to pick up the slack, it might be a wise investment to buy a portable computer with fax capabilities that could be checked out by any team member as needed. If the work that Sue is doing must be done at the office, investigate together whether or not it would be possible to swap parts of the work with someone else whose tasks do not necessarily require being at the office. This is a chance for some team brainstorming. There is no need to go into this meeting thinking you have to have all the answers. The process of sharing ideas together could lead to the development of some imaginative measures. Invite the group to throw all their ideas on the table and reassure them that no idea is too farfetched.

It is most important that this meeting end with two outcomes. The first one should be some immediate solutions that will help Sue. While the plans could be applied to any of you, they will be applied specifically to Sue in the immediate future. The second outcome should be some long range ideas that you will develop into a draft contingency plan to be reviewed as soon as the current situation is resolved.

Guilt and anger are real and understandable emotions being felt by the rest of the team as they struggle to deal with the level of job stress being experienced, and the fact that one member is unable to contribute as fully as is needed just at this time. Be honest with the team about what they are feeling and acknowledge that their responses are normal and understandable. There is nothing wrong with feeling the emotions, the issue is how those emotions are handled. If the team has not been exposed to methods for peaceful conflict resolution, it might be wise to schedule some training in the process as soon as the crunch is over.

A word about guilt and anger...

Helping your staff to move past what could potentially be an example of discrimination based on gender and marital status and on to a clearer vision of teamwork will only reap positive benefits throughout your department.

CRUNCHING MANAGEMENT

For eight years you have worked at the Sweetdreams Hotel in the Housekeeping Department. Your primary responsibilities have been to work as part of a team that cleans rooms, changes linen, vacuums, etc. Supervision has been provided by a Rooms' Manager who would each day assign you and the other housekeepers a list of rooms to be done, and then monitor your progress throughout the day. You have an excellent attendance record, a reputation for doing good work and you get along well with the other employees.

One day, after work, the hotel manager asks to see you. You learn that the manager has recently been to a conference on the New Organizational Structure (NOS) *and has determined that the hotel has too many managers. The NOS approach to management is based on the premise that across the nation middle-management positions are being eliminated, with responsibility and authority being pushed down to the lowest levels possible.*

The cleaning of rooms will no longer be done under a manager who decides who will change linens, who will vacuum, who will be responsible for which rooms and so on. That organizational position and that person are being removed from the hotel staffing structure. What you are now told is that you are to be the team leader of a seven-person team, and that "...as associates of this company your seven-person team is responsible for the proper preparation of rooms for our guests. Your team has the third through the eleventh floors. You, as team leader, decide in cooperation with your team who does what chores and how to best divide the labor. Of course, if you can't handle the responsibility, we will have to find someone who can. I really want to push for these self-directed teams, and I am sure that your excellent record of performance will continue under this new structure. We'll switch over in about one week, so you have a few days to talk it over with your team and sort things out. Good luck!"

How do you start? What do you do during the next few days to get ready for the new structure and your new role? What can you do to provide the greatest chance to succeed?

Will the Peter Principle show up?

Well, congratulations. This scenario could go one of several ways. But with the time, training and preparation you have been given to properly assume this new set of responsibilities you may very well end up being the latest candidate for at least night sweats if not an ulcer. This is the essence of the Peter Principle, the concept of personnel being promoted beyond their levels of competence. A little brutal honesty is called for: You have not been promoted to this position on the basis of any solid management skills. Now you are told that in a week you must organize personnel, understand the concepts of time management, oversee equipment and handle some budgetary concerns. Finally, although you are now everyone's good buddy, you are about to be making decisions about the working conditions of your friends, mediating their conflicts with you and each other and possibly making hiring and firing decisions. And you're supposed to be able to step in and have this all working tiptop in one short week. Good luck. Your chances for failure are high.

Don't panic. Take a deep breath and keep reading. This is do-able, but it will take some readjusting of your current mindset. First things first. It is obviously up to you to break the news to the rest of your work team. It does not appear that you're going to get much help with that all too important part of this transition. You can reasonably expect some jealousy, anger and distrust from all the other team members who also show up on time, do a good job and are friendly. You have been promoted over them and may even be seeing more money in your paycheck than was there before. There has been no announcement that change of this sort was coming nor any opportunity to apply for the position. Your appointment over them is going to seem arbitrary. Unfortunately, this awkward and difficult situation is the one you have inherited. You have some tough ethical decisions to make. You can decide the hassle isn't worth it and simply walk away, or you can pull yourself up and decide that you will make the best of it. We will continue on the presumption that you choose to stick with it.

Go buy some muffins and coffee.

Go buy some muffins and coffee. Show up early the next day and as the rest of the team comes in invite them to sit down with you. There is something you have to tell them. Make it clear from the beginning that the decision is a "given" for all of you. You are to become an independent team and will be making decisions about how the work gets done among yourselves. Let them know that you have been asked to facilitate the team process, but it is your intent that not much will change because you're going to be doing what you've always done only now the team will be self-managed.

Place as little emphasis as possible on the fact that you have been placed in charge. The fact that you are the one bringing the news to them will make that clear enough. Your primary objective in this meeting must be to alleviate their concerns that you are still one of the team. Remember that in the past, as you have worked together, you have all shared secrets, gossip, bickering, jokes and personal issues. Without having to say it, you need to make it clear right from the start that the interpersonal relationships are still in place and that they can trust you. You are not going to use any personal information to sabotage them. This is important because the potential for their sabotaging you could become an issue if you are not sensitive to their feelings.

Okay, so your approach should be "Good grief, there is major reshuffling going on. They want us to organize into an independent team. What would be some better ways to do what we've been doing?" Again, without ever saying so, it is clear that you are in charge. All that has to happen now is effectively implementing the structure you have been given, which is effectively no structure other than "Go for it." What your team has been doing is obviously acceptable, the rooms have been cleaned, the customers are happy. Your team members might have some good ideas to help make your time on task even more effective. Ask them to keep track of their ideas, share them with you and implement any that are reasonable. If the higher-ups pay your team a compliment that has to do with one of their suggestions, make sure you let them know from whom the idea came. Ethically, you will look like the good team player you are and one of your team members might also be promoted on the basis of that information.

Once you actually get started, ask everyone to keep either mental or written notes of solutions to problems or good ideas that occur to them. Ask them how often they feel it is important to meet to talk about issues that might arise. You may be thinking that once a week sounds reasonable and they want to meet every two weeks. Go with it. If the agendas are lengthy after two weeks or ideas get lost in that time, ask them if they want to meet more often. As much as possible, make decisions as a team. Listen carefully to their input. Express your concerns, but unless they suggest something as obviously unacceptable as cleaning rooms only once every other day, try their ideas out. Remember all the other floors in this hotel are also going to be cleaned by independent teams. Certain levels of competition are inevitable, so it is very unlikely that any team member is going to come up with an idea that will make you look bad.

It seems like this will be a pretty straightforward transition. No problem, unless of course you are in charge of evaluating the performance of your team. If that is the case, the fact that you are now the evaluator is what will generate the highest levels of distrust. However, your team understands performance criteria. Rooms need to be cleaned and comfortable so that when guests enter or reenter them they will feel relatively at home. Discuss with your team the ways to successfully fulfill these expectations. If the rooms are clean and the guests are content, the team would be judged to be working effectively. If you can all agree that these are reasonable standards, then there is no need for you to be in charge of judging the quality of work done by other team members.

When you can catch the ear of your manager for five seconds, one point that does need to be clarified is whether or not you are to report a problem that arises with another employee. Simply ask what you should do if there is a concern. Should you pass it along or handle it internally? If you are asked to pass the information along, make that information clear to the rest of your team. It is out of your hands and is one of the "givens." If the expectation is for you to handle problems internally, let the team know that as well. As a team, work to develop the method by which problems will be handled. Let them know that your only concerns are that problems be addressed quickly, fairly and confidentially.

A logical follow-up to this process is working with the rest of the team to develop some conflict resolution and mediation skills. If a problem between team members arises it would be wise for them to have strategies in place that will help to peacefully confront and resolve problems as they occur, as opposed to holding a grudge until it erupts and you find yourself drawn into it. Your reasoning for this is that you are still a seven-member team with approximately the same workload as before. In order to remain efficient, your time cannot be spent listening to gripes and taking on the problems of others. Let the team know that you want to continue as a fully contributing member of the team's success, and that they need to be proactive in their interpersonal working relationships so you can use your time well.

And then get going. Let everyone know they are a well-functioning team and that just the tiniest bit of adjustment might be needed to make the transition a successful prospect. Avoid throwing your weight around, don't let the promotion go to your head and keep your eye on the ball.

WHAT ABOUT ROBERT?

Robert has been a reliable employee for many years. He is part of a staff that you supervise that works rather well as

When you can catch the ear of your manager for five seconds...

a team, and the number and type of personnel problems you are called upon to handle are few and usually minor.

About four months ago, Robert and his wife lost a child to leukemia. It was a difficult, stressful time for him and his family and the staff were as supportive as possible. Robert took some time off following the funeral and has now been back on the job for a little over two months.

Sometime after returning to work, Robert came to you and told you that he was at peace with what had happened because he and his wife had found greater strength since their loss by becoming much more active in their religion. He seemed to be deriving comfort from this involvement and you stated that you were pleased he and his wife were recovering from their loss.

Now, a few weeks later, you received a request from several of your employees to have lunch with them. After some nervous small talk, an employee burst out with "Robert is driving us crazy! He is forever telling us about the peace and happiness he and his wife have found, and what a great thing his religion has done for them. We are genuinely sorry about what happened, and if he can be healed through his religion that is wonderful, but, well...." Another employee finishes "... we just don't want to hear about it anymore."

"Robert is driving us crazy!"

You ask whether Robert has been proselytizing, or in any way trying to get his fellow employees to join his faith or even be more active in their own. But he has not; the only problem is that he is repeating himself at every opportunity, and no one wants to tell him that enough is enough. However, he is annoying his co-workers, and they feel strained and embarrassed by the situation. They ask you to talk to Robert. To build toward better relations in the future, they want you to do it without mentioning specific names of those who complained.

You feel that they—not you—should speak to him as a friend, and explain how they feel. Problems: Will they think you are ducking your rightful role as manager if you refuse to talk to him? Or, if they talk to him, will they mishandle the situation, cause hard feelings, and underscore their belief that you should have spoken to Robert in the first place?

Perhaps you should suggest things for them to say or for them to avoid saying? What to do?

This is really not a big problem. It is a minor irritation among workers. The first thing you have to ask yourself is how much minute detail do you want to be involved in? Do you want to micro- or macro-manage? If you want to micro-manage every concern any employee might ever have with any other employee, then by all means talk to Robert. You will be sending your employees the clear message that they have neither the brains nor the people skills to effectively deal with Robert's continued conversation about his beliefs, and that you are the only one who knows how to handle the situation. Once you have so effectively disempowered your workers be prepared for your inbasket to fill up while you rush around the plant soothing every wounded ego and settling every petty argument that might arise at any time in the future. What a waste of time and energy!

Begin by asking yourself "Who owns the problem?" You clearly do not and you want to be careful not to take ownership of it for all the reasons stated above. You need to help your employees understand the issues, understand why it is they and not you who should talk to Robert, and practice a few strategies to help ensure that that talk will be productive. You do not want to tell them what to say. That is as disempowering an idea as is talking to Robert yourself. You do want to present them with some ideas and be a participant in their practice session to prepare for the conversation with Robert.

First of all, they need to understand the issues. Robert is not proselytizing. Even if he were, within the appropriate time, place and manner, that should not be a problem. But he is not. He is simply recounting over and over again a single theme. If he were recalling an old war story, or telling a tiresome joke endlessly, the situation would be much the same. Help your employees to put this in perspective. It is not about religion, but about interpersonal relations.

Secondly, work with this group to help them appreciate their role in the problem. Let them know you understand that this situation can indeed be irritating and you are interested in helping them explore and practice techniques that will bring about a resolution with which everyone can be comfortable. If they ask you to talk to Robert, decline with a smile. Let them know that Robert will forever wonder who went behind his back to management and that distrust rather than friendship will be cemented if they do not bring their concerns to him themselves.

Here again is where ongoing staff development in conflict resolution and problem solving would have settled the issue before it ever came your way. But it's never too late. If you don't understand how it works, hire a consultant for a training session or two. Encourage the employees who came to you to see you after the session, and work together to synthesize the problem-solving techniques into a specific approach for this situation. They might decide to sit down together with Robert, or for each of them to speak to Robert when the problem comes his or her way. Be supportive and express your sincere belief that they are capable of finding a resolution that will leave dignity and working relations intact. No one will accuse you of ducking your responsibilities if you explain to them why you should not be the one to approach Robert and then facilitate their encounter with him. In the long run, the staff development and guidance you provide now will result in undisturbed time later for attending to the inbox.

FIRST AMENDMENT RIGHTS AND COLOGNE

Last week you hired a new clerk to work in an office shared by several other people, each at their own desks. The employee started on Monday; today is Friday. During the week you had three complaints about this person wearing a strong cologne. You made a point of visiting today and found the complaints to be accurate. In your opinion it would be annoying to have to sit near this employee for eight hours a day.

This scenario contains a number of issues which we have already touched upon but, nevertheless, they will help to further illustrate how the language of time, place and manner can be used during daily interactions in the workplace. The other issue to be examined is the development of professional style. One of the problems most new managers have is that they have the desire to manage everything. Any problem that comes their way appears to be theirs to solve. As a new manager, unsure of how to act,

You had three complaints about this person wearing a strong cologne.

you waited a full week and listened to three complaints before walking by the employee and deciding her perfume might indeed be too strong. Now you feel the need to act, but action should have come much sooner.

When using a democratic form of management, the first response to a problem is to ask yourself, "What needs to be learned here?" Do employees need to learn that their First Amendment rights can be arbitrarily taken away if some fellow workers find their manner of free expression offensive? The decision you are faced with is to leap into this fray and teach your employees that going behind the back of fellow workers will reap some interesting rewards. Or you may want to consider helping your staff to learn that when they encounter a problem there are legal considerations to be weighed and ethical practices to be employed that will resolve the situation in a cooperative and respectful manner.

When the first complaint came in, you should have encouraged the employee to go directly to the clerk. It is, after all, a problem between the two of them. If the employee had expressed uncertainties over how to approach the problem, an empowering manager should have spent time with this person brainstorming some strategies for approaching the clerk. First, the employee should be reminded that the clerk is engaging in a First Amendment expression. With that in mind, how can the employee express his or her concerns to the clerk in a way that will preserve personal freedoms and not be offensive? It may very well be that in the course of this brainstorming session the employee will realize that the problem is his or hers and that nothing should be said or done. Perhaps all that is needed is to exercise tolerance for personal expression.

But, if the employee is convinced an impasse exists and is still not comfortable confronting the clerk alone, you can offer to serve as a mediator for the meeting. Serving as a mediator will allow you to play a totally objective role in a process that is designed for problem solving. What you must not do is offer to serve as a mediator and then, during the meeting, be the one suggesting solutions.

If you choose to hear three complaints, let the problem grow and then assume the responsibility of determining whether or not the cologne is offensive, you are in effect saying to all employees, "This office rewards those who go behind the backs of others," or worse, "This company does not believe its adult employees can decide when there really is a problem and lacks confidence that they have the skills to resolve it." Neither message is useful when trying to build a work environment that reflects trust and respect.

If, and when, other complaints come in, you should take a posture of equanimity. It may be that these three employees don't like the clerk for whatever reason. By going and "sniffing out the problem," you are appearing to side with them. You must make it very clear that your job is to protect the clerk's rights of personal expression while helping to maintain a healthy and safe work environment. After working with the first complainant to develop strategies for resolving the problem, you need to sit back and give these strategies time to work.

If no progress is being made in a week or two, or even if great strides are accomplished, you should bring the issue before the next meeting of the site-management team. As with the situation involving the burning of incense, there may be ways to resolve conflicts such as this by developing guidelines for time, place and manner.

TO WAGE OR NOT TO WAGE

Your company of fifteen hundred employees consists of one factory with nine hundred hourly productions employees;

three hundred hourly employees in testing, maintenance, clerical and other positions; and three hundred salaried employees working as administrative assistants, or in sales and management positions. The workforce is non-union, sales are good, employee morale appears to be high, turnover is low and the company is respected in the marketplace. You are the personnel manager.

For some time, the company has been working to install democratic concepts such as Team Building, Quality Circles and Every Employee An Inspector. Implementation of these concepts has appeared to go smoothly.

Part One. One day the company president asks to see you. After reviewing the success you have been experiencing with the other strategies, she says, "I want to bounce an idea off you and ask that you give it some serious thought and come back to me with your comments."

"It seems to me that we have a sort of double standard here . . . that we are spending a lot of time and effort in building one big team, one unified family, but we persist in having hourly and salary employees, non-exempt and exempt. The hourly employees have to punch time clocks and get doctors' excuses when they are out more than three days on sick leave and we don't. It is almost as though we don't trust them, or assume that they need those controls and punishments, like docking pay for being late. At the same time we want them to be fully responsible as equals in building the company."

The president leans forward in her chair. "What I want you to tell me is what happens if we make everyone salaried. . . . no time clocks . . . the same sick leave and vacation rules for everyone. Is this too optimistic? Will it help us build a better team? What are the potential risks? Please prepare a report for me as soon as possible."

We have a sort of double standard here . . .

How do you handle this assignment? What are the political gains and losses? What are the key items of your report? What is your recommendation? Keep the present system or go to all salaried employees? Why?

Part 2. It is now six months later. Based on your wonderful report the company became totally salaried three months ago. The transition appeared to go smoothly and morale seems to be high.

The only problem is that a small group of the former hourly employees seem to be testing the limits of the system. They come to work five to ten minutes late or stay an extra ten minutes at lunch. Since much of the production work depends on teams or multi-step production lines, the absence of one person can affect several others. In some cases peer pressure has been brought to bear. You are pleased that this strategy seemed to work since in those cases the urging to be prompt came not from upper management but from the person's own co-workers.

There are, however, a few employees who seem to be not responding well to the comments from co-workers. You are concerned that this is a potential source of trouble, and that other employees are becoming upset by their co-workers "getting away" with poor attitudes. What do you do?

Well, certainly this scenario seems to paint a bright picture of a company where everyone is very happy. While we despair at being seen as cynical, we would begin by encouraging the president and the personnel manager to remove their rose-colored glasses. The fact is that while this company might be a great employer for salaried personnel, it might be quite the opposite for those receiving hourly wages.

One of our first clues that something might be awry is the way this new plan was created, that is behind the closed doors of an administrative office. While the president's intentions are certainly honorable, and we would be the last to fault the desire to make this workplace more equitable, what is being demonstrated here is what can happen when democratic strategies are imposed over a relatively autocratic method of operation.

If all the other innovations now in place were originally planned in secret, without the input of a site team, you can bet that all is not well out on the floor of the plant. No matter how empowering the new strategy might potentially turn out to be, if its impetus comes from closed-door meetings attended only by upper-level management, workers will tend to view the resulting change as "one more thing to do." In addition, the concepts that have been implemented so far have to do with peers supervising peers. Workers may see this as a good thing, or they may see it as a way for management to pass the buck down the line for performance evaluation. Rather than building team spirit and trust, the act of imposing these innovations on employees who have no training in peer supervision may well have created a tense environment where the workers are consumed with watching their backs. The point we are trying to make here is that a memo from on high that announces something like "Guess what, we're all going to be democratic now," is probably not going to be met with wild enthusiasm.

Transitions that are this profound must be accompanied by careful thought, shared planning and plant-wide retraining. While the earlier changes have created some marked differences, the latest plan is going to probably result in some fear that the method or amount of payment will be different. The closer these changes come to the pocketbook, the more you can count on an elevated level of concern. Without an opportunity to carefully lay the foundation for this change or to provide workers an opportunity for input into how the new structure might work, a system of payment which could result in some very positive outcomes throughout the worksite may fail.

Let's take a closer look at exactly why this change is being batted around. The president is saying ". . . we are spending a lot of time and effort in building one big team, one unified family, but we persist in having hourly and salary employees, non-exempt and exempt. The hourly employees have to punch time clocks and get doctors' excuses when they are out more than three days on sick leave and we don't. It is almost like we don't trust them, or assume that they need those controls and punishments, like docking pay for being late. At the same time we want them to be fully responsible as equals in building the company." Her own words frame an attitude that is not uncommon among managers, that is talking about democracy while continuing the status quo. Democratic management has to be underpinned by trust and respect to be effective. Her comment about the old two-tiered system having the appearance of not trusting workers could easily be responded to with a deafening "No kidding."

The wages/salary structure inevitably has contributed to the creation of some distrust among the employees. It's a good bet that those workers who are paid by the hour have become very good at survival skills that probably include lying over the phone about who is really sick at home, who is on vacation and about almost any other aspect of this system that requires deception to make it work for them. This company has institutionalized a structure that would logically result in the use of wide spread deception by making a distinction between what is or what is not an "excused absence" for only one set of workers.

The glimmer of hope that attitudes can change and everything can be made better lies in the fact that those in charge seem to understand that they are acting in ways that appear to be contradictory. Management has continued for too long to depend on policies that treat workers like children, encouraging lying and punishing them when they are bad. The president's last sentence sums up the problems looming on the horizon when she says, "At the same time we want them to be fully responsible as equals in building the company." This is like a parent telling a child to be responsible. Responsible behavior cannot be imposed. Responsibility presents itself as an intrinsic response in an individual who is treated with trust and respect. There is more work to be done.

You view having the president ask your opinion as your chance to shine. But move carefully here. There is a lot of work to be done to prepare workers for the sort of transition that is being planned. You want to present a plan that will provide for systematic training which will include peer mediation, conflict resolution and trust building strategies. Be cautious. Political games being what they are, it is wise to set up a program that can be implemented by your president. You never want to embarrass your administrator, so you need to educate her in order to have her prepared to effectively facilitate the training of everyone else in the worksite.

Priority must be placed on trust building among the two groups of employees. Because the hourly workers have in all likelihood incorporated deception into their work culture, your worksite probably includes one group with little or nothing to gain by being dishonest with management, and another group with a history of all sorts of positive outcomes resulting from the telling of a lie or two. Your first task is to get everyone on the same page in terms of their ethical view of the working environment. However, sitting the hourly workers down to a lecture on ethics while the rest of the employees go about their business will only exacerbate the dual standard rather than fix it.

It does not appear that this plant currently has a site team in place. This would definitely be the time to get one set up and functioning. And yes, it should be made up of representatives from both groups. Their first task would be to investigate, discuss and plan training sessions for and implementation of effective strategies for trust building in your particular worksite. It is important to get a firm grasp on the idea that the transition to a worksite employing only salaried workers deserves to take time. The faster you move, the more you leave yourself open to careless oversights that could very well result in injured feelings and misunderstandings. Slow down, and move thoughtfully.

The more time you spend on training and creating a mindset for trust, the fewer problems you will have when you actually switch over. Be prepared to honestly discuss the mistakes of the past and the distrust and deception that has resulted. Help them to understand that they are not the only ones going through a transition, management is as well. Make it clear that everyone will be participating in the training sessions together, and that everyone should be open to new ideas. The new policies are not something being done to one group which has already been on the receiving end of some undesirable decisions, but rather the innovations will occur as a shared experience. Your biggest challenge will be to help your president understand that the change will only result in democratic outcomes if the transition is accomplished in an equally open, democratic environment.

Six months later the less productive behaviors of a small group of former hourly employees are an unfortunate result of the culture you have but are now working to change. You are being tested. Every employee who drifts in late, lingers over lunch or dawdles back from a coffee break is probably asking you the same question, "Do you really mean it?" Just because you have publicly announced that now everyone is going to be a happy equal doesn't necessarily make it so. Your employees are far more thoroughly schooled in the old climate of double standards than they are in the current wave of equity washing over the site.

The single worst strategy you can use is the reliance on peer pressure to fix the attitudes. To do so is to leave some potentially serious disagreements in the hands of workers who probably lack the skills to peacefully resolve problems in ways that will serve the best interests of your company. If you still think the use of peer pressure would be a good idea, ask yourself what form the peer pressure will take? Do you want workers to control each other by scolding, making snide remarks or chastising in ways that will create irreparable rifts? You may see peer pressure "working" but you have to go on to ask, "Working towards what end?" On the other hand, turning the same problems over to trained peer mediators, if the site team believes that is the best way to handle such issues, will at least give you the probability of these behaviors being resolved in ways that will help, not hinder, the working environment.

Resist the pressure that might exist to have co-workers punished for the behaviors they are exhibiting. This is a step backwards and will not help in any way to foster the democratic spirit you are seeking. If you believe that there is value in democratic practices then you have to be willing to establish and stick to policies that consistently model respect for each individual worker. Punitive measures can only support the authoritative policies you are trying to move beyond. Punishment is done to people, and the ones being punished are left being passive recipients of the decisions being made for them. Their ability to make better decisions than they are making now is not enhanced by this process. So don't allow yourself to be drawn into a reactive sort of leadership. You know going into this that there will be some who will test the new system, so prepare for it. Train your peer mediators before you need them. Teach conflict resolution skills before you have people angry with each other, and stand firm. This transition will only be successful if the model you establish as a leader makes a clear statement through every decision that you will be striving hard to ensure each individual's success.

Those workers who are calling for punishment must be helped to understand that you are no longer operating under standards that will satisfy some workers at the expense of others. The best way to do that is to not even think about docking an employee for being late, because if you do decide to take such actions you will in effect be announcing to every worker that the change is only superficial and that you really do not trust them to function responsibly without the threat of punishment. And once they get that message you might as well reinstitute hourly wages and the old two-tiered system, because the new approach has been negated. You have been appointed a leader in this change process; assume the leadership role with grace.

Those workers who are challenging the system may require some one-on-one conferences with you. There may be some personal problems occurring in their lives about which you are unaware. They may need some help with time management skills. They may need some peer mediation to help them work through problems with co-workers. The point is you will never find out what the problem is with an arbitrary blanket policy of docking wages.

Instituting this change is worth all the effort you give to it. The equity that will result isn't just a good idea, it's good business.

PERVASIVE VULGARITY?

As a manager of a factory with over three thousand employees, it is impossible for you to know all of the workers by name, or to visit all of their workstations, although you do get out onto the factory floor with some regularity. Part of the operation involves highly skilled workers who produce special tools, jigs, dies, gauges and other pieces of equipment. Not only do they produce for internal use, but a large part of their activity is creating parts for smaller companies who buy from your firm.

All of the craftsmen are males, who work for the most part in individual cubicles. They are visited by other craftsmen in need of assistance, and occasionally by sales representatives who are asking questions about delivery of a part. All of your sales staff is male, and all have engineering degrees, in order that they might act as consultants as well as salesmen. You have men and women in the front office to handle billing, payroll and various accounting and clerical functions. It is rare that they visit any of the production workers, but may do so periodically to clarify a billing question.

An incident of sexual harassment towards a woman occurs at another facility owned by the parent firm. The woman sues and the company loses. A memo comes out from the home office restating the company's non-discrimination policy and urging that all employees be aware of and avoid offensive attitudes and behavior. A copy is sent to everyone in the firm.

The next day one of your front office employees comes in to complain about the calendars one of the craftsmen has in his cubicle. She states that she has long been offended by them, that they are sexist and that they demean women and portray them as sex objects. She further states that the memo has encouraged her to speak out, that she is glad she works for such a decent company and is sure you will do the right thing. You promise to investigate.

When you stop by to visit the employee, you see three calendars provided by vending companies. Each has a picture of a pretty young woman posing in a skimpy bathing suit. While they are not works of art, neither are they, in your judgment, in any way obscene. The women are portrayed as sex objects, but the photos represent what could be seen at a public beach. After a casual chat, you return to your office. For whatever reason, the company personnel manual does not address the question of individual decoration of one's workspace.

It is your belief that the woman is sincere and truly offended by the pictures. However, they are not at her workstation, but in a cubicle that she rarely visits. You are sure that other similar posters and calendars exist in the factory.

Do you deny her request, and if so, with what explanation? Do you invoke a policy that calls for the removal of all such pictures? If you do, how do you state your reasons? And where is the line drawn: Can a man display a picture of a woman in a short skirt? Can he have a picture on his desk of a woman in a bathing suit if that woman is his wife? Can *a woman display a picture of her male partner wearing shorts and no shirt?*

If you call for the removal of posters and calendars, you will most likely have several workers file a grievance. If you deny the woman's request, she may go over your head to corporate administration, which is highly sensitive at this time. Whatever you choose, you will have to have your reasons well-thought-out and be prepared to defend them.

Once again, there are a number of legal as well as ethical issues popping up in this story. The first question you need to ask is why certain employees seem to be hired to fill specific roles? The fact that all sales personnel are male and that women appear only in the front office may or may not be a coincidence. You need to review your hiring practices and ensure that the most competent person is being hired to fill various roles around the plant. Gender discrimination in hiring practices is a Fourteenth Amendment issue. It may be that the person from the front office, who brings the complaint to you, is responding as much to her position in the plant as she is to the calendar pictures. If she suspects that she will never climb the corporate ladder because and only because of her gender, her anger and frustration may have been seeking an outlet. The calendars may have provided a convenient opportunity for her to raise the issues about which she is really concerned.

Your next step is to investigate what, if any, company policy exists dealing with displays of posters or calendars. Find out if the company has established definitions for such vague terms as "offensive attitudes and behavior." Although the situation will need to be handled in your shop, you should seek support and clarification from the parent firm. Copy a letter of your request to the woman who came to you with her concerns, and add a hand written note on the bottom thanking her for bringing this matter to your attention. That will buy you some time to think through your next moves.

This story could go one of two ways depending on whether the parent company has a stated policy dealing with pervasive vulgarity in the workplace. If their policy sets out a specific rule stating that no posters and/or calendars may be displayed at workstations, then not to require their removal in your shop is to be insubordinate. You have no decision to make. This is called a "given."

In the United States, law is generated from four sources: the Constitution, which represents individual rights; legislation, representing majority interests; case law, which resolves and clarifies existing law and disputes; and administrative law, which is created by businesses and institutions to serve their special needs. If the parent firm has an administrative law that specifically bans the kind of photograph in question, then the manager in this scenario must implement that policy and the items in question must go.

But for the sake of argument, let us assume that the parent firm responds to your request by stating that they have no specific policy, they just want everyone to be nice to everyone else.

A manager who wishes to be known as democratic must move very carefully in this situation. There are a number of issues involved that could blow up in anyone's face. First of all, when dress, slogans, pictures, etc. are banned from public institutions, most commonly schools, it is generally because they have been found to be either pervasively vulgar or of such a nature that they have been known to create a pattern of serious disruption. Recent school rules banning the wearing of certain football team jackets because of a pattern that links the wearing of such jackets to gang activity would be one example of how this concept is applied.

In this case, however, we are probably dealing with what might be pervasive vulgarity. Pervasive vulgarity has been defined as "I know it when I see it," so there is a great deal of leeway in determining what may or may not fit this category. For the purposes of this book, the legal questions in this case play a secondary role to the ethical issues of how safe and supportive female employees perceive their work environment to be.

Whether or not the calendars are pervasively vulgar, or are indeed representations of what can be seen on public beaches is not the issue here. Rather, the issue is how to mediate the conflict between these two employees so that neither is alienated. As the manager in this scenario, you are strongly advised to take a critical look at the whole environment. If female employees perceive themselves to be victims of harassment that is represented or actively encouraged by the presence of calendar pinups, you must take action.

If the parent company has no clear-cut policy, the manager should work two ways to resolve the conflict. First, call a meeting of all workers. Talk about the incident in general terms while avoiding the mention of specific names. Apologize for not taking action sooner, and let them know that your door is open to hear all views. Assemble your site-management team to review the issues. Ask the team to compile information on the extent of the concerns. In the interim, pending a ruling from the parent firm, and based on complaints received, your policy will be that calendar pinups are pervasively vulgar and, therefore, seriously disruptive to the workplace environment. As for pictures on desks, the issue will still be pervasive vulgarity. Provide your workers, no matter where they are situated or what their jobs, with some general guidelines for what is or is not considered to be pervasively vulgar in your plant, then let them make their own judgments as to which pictures, calendars or posters they will display. Empowering them to judge if their photographs could be considered offensive is to treat them as responsible adults and remove yourself from the stress of being embroiled in endless decisions on each separate item a worker might want to hang up.

At the same time as you are putting out the fires in your plant, you should also be sending a memo to the parent company clearly outlining the problems you are encountering in your workplace and how you are handling the situation. Request that they develop a clear, evenhanded approach to workstations as well as hiring practices so that in the future similar problems may not arise.

Once policy has been established in your plant, follow it up with a visit to every workstation in your facility. If, as you walk by a workstation, you spot a picture which a reasonable person might believe to be pervasively vulgar, stop a moment for a quiet conference. As always, begin with an I-Message and try to help the employee understand another perspective of the situation. Be prepared to follow up with this employee in private conferences using counseling strategies discussed in earlier scenarios. Be patient. Some workers will not be prepared to change immediately. Let them know that they are important to the success of the plant, and assist them in understanding the perspective of another person.

In the final analysis, any worker's right to equal protection is paramount, and freedom from harassment of any kind should be a standard that is constantly strived for in the workplace. Education is a vital component in this process and should be used to help all workers understand that as you protect each of them, you protect all of them.

NEW MANAGER—TOUGH ASSIGNMENT

You have recently been hired to supervise a customer service department with a staff of 25 in a large insurance firm. The work consists of answering phone calls and letters that deal with customers' policies. The items being dealt with may be fairly simple, such as a change of address or beneficiary, or may involve research of certain benefits and financial information. In the latter case, the customer is usually responded to by letter, although occasionally by a return phone call.

The office hours are 8:30 A.M. to 5:30 P.M. with a one-hour lunch. The phones are controlled by the main switchboard to ring from 9:00 A.M. to 5:00 P.M. The extra half hour on each end is designed to allow for paperwork, cleaning up old business without interruption and as a freedom from the ringing phones. While it is not the highest pressure office situation, the calls are fairly constant.

Your boss, upon hiring you, informs you that customer satisfaction is not as high as the company desires. The company often sends out questionnaires to people who have received service. Recent surveys have indicated a growing problem with errors, late responses and a general slipping of quality. It is made quite clear to you that your career depends on the department making an immediate and significant improvement.

The personnel files you inherit contain little except hire dates and a few general comments. You are going to have to learn all the names, and the talents, skills and problems that go with those names, quickly.

This is what you observe:

1. *Most of the staff comes in around 8:20 A.M. to 8:25 A.M., gets coffee and visits. A few people come in between 8:30 A.M. and 8:40 A.M. While there is some work done during the half hour before 9:00 A.M., you guess that you are getting about two-thirds work value, about twenty minutes of being on task.*

2. *After the phones stop ringing, there is a definite let down. While people do clean up unfinished business, you know that you are not getting full value.*

3. *Between the first half hour and the last, at a loss of ten minutes of productivity each, times twenty-five employees, you are losing five hundred minutes of work, the equivalent of eight hours of work per day.*

On the other hand . . .

The job is stressful, with constant phone calls, confused and occasionally angry clients. Your employees have to patiently explain the same regulations over and over. Workers have to complete paperwork, while sitting looking at display terminals for hours. People sometimes get burned out. Therefore, the half hours at the start and end of the day may be in fact psychologically, and even physiologically necessary.

Achieving an effective balance between the soft and hard activities of your people.

So you must determine, and quickly, what is going on and what the solutions are. Is everyone overworked? Do you need more staff? Is everyone goofing off? How can you find these things out without offending your workers, or building hostility or suspicion? How do you tighten up, if that is what is needed, in a responsible fashion? Or are there more creative solutions to this problem?

As the new manager you are already in trouble. A situation beyond your control is occurring and must be acted upon quickly. While it is always wise for a new administrator to get a feel for a setting before changing anything, operating from the premise that "if it ain't broke, don't fix it," your new position does not allow you this luxury. Begin instead by calling your new staff together in order to set out introductory information of your vision for a democratic work environment. Let workers know that you are glad to be onboard and that you are all one team. Verbalize a good deal of empathy for the jobs they do and compliment them on the quality they are maintaining.

Do not, as a first move, go through personnel files. Every worker knows that there have been customer complaints. Grapevines in any organization are kept buzzing all the time with such tidbits. If your first move is to ask your secretary for placement files, you can estimate that that information will be well-circulated before the first coffee break.

Whatever your intentions might be for reviewing them, this is not the way to build trust. If your employees don't trust you, they will sabotage you. If this is your first move, you can expect a career change before very long. If you want to find out about them, schedule a series of meetings with small groups, so that most phones remain functional while you are getting acquainted with your staff.

What you need at this point is some help focusing on issues. As is the problem with many people new to authority, you are getting distracted by red herrings. The concern in this division is not time on task, but customer satisfaction. As manager you need to take a more global view, relax about the ticking clock and try a little creativity. There are no legal issues here, but certainly ethical concerns will come into play. First of all, stop trying to manage everything. You may have become convinced that whatever solutions can be found must come from you. What you are forgetting is that these employees have been doing this job for some time and probably have some good ideas of how to streamline the process. But no one has asked for their opinions, or they have been asked but their responses were not acted upon. Either way they are probably feeling disempowered, and the lack of personal ownership over their work environment is contributing to their slowed productivity.

A manager who wishes to create a democratic work environment is an individual who believes in personal empowerment. Let your workers know that you are all in this lifeboat together, and you need their help. Be honest and straightforward with them. Develop a site-management team with input from the staff. Remind the team of the company's goals and any "givens" that must be considered during their deliberations. When they make suggestions, **act upon those ideas.** If the ideas they generate pose some problems, work with the site team to correct the difficulties, but do not abandon their useful suggestions.

More staff is not necessarily the answer. If, after the new ideas have been tried, it is evident that new personnel are still needed, then do the hiring. But if the problems stem from job dissatisfaction, not overwork, new staff will only fall into the patterns of old staff and not much will change. Be willing to try any reasonable notion suggested by your site team, and while new ideas are being implemented, do not make the mistake of hiding in your office. Be out and about the shop. Ask for lots of feedback as ideas are tried. Pick up a ringing phone and attempt to answer a question or two. Demonstrate in every word and deed that you are a team working together to correct whatever problems exist.

As change occurs, there will be grumbling. New situations can be very frightening to some people and they will need your support, encouragement and understanding as they work through the uncertainties that might accompany restructuring. Be patient. Put yourself in their shoes and realize how difficult it can be to suddenly alter old routines. If you can hang in there through the rough spots, you will find more and more of them moving with you.

Some may choose to leave because they are having difficulty identifying their place in the new scheme of things.

Give them your best wishes as they go. When you replace them, interview each new candidate with an eye toward how this person will fit into the team. Ask questions that require the candidate to problem solve. Invite site-management teammembers to join in the interview, and give each an equal voice in recommending to you who should be hired.

LITERACY IN THE WORKPLACE

You are the manager of a factory with about one thousand employees. It is one of seven owned by the parent company. The factory is old, with a lot of antiquated equipment. Business is good and the factory runs fairly well, but the equipment is starting to become a problem. Other plants in the company chain are starting to regularly out-produce your own. Rumors of a plant closing have circulated for years.

The ages of the employees are not evenly distributed. Ten years ago there was an extensive layoff that lasted for over five years, and when the company started hiring in the past few years, few of the former employees were rehired. Since your plant pays well there were many applications for employment, and the company decided to hire only those who had at least graduated from high school.

Thus, your employees are divided into two groups. The largest group, roughly two-thirds of your total personnel, range in age from eighteen to their mid-thirties. The remaining third of the workforce are in their mid-forties and up.

The two groups have gotten along well, but for the most part the two groups do not mix. They do not tend to eat lunch or go out after work with anyone but those in their own groups. In general, you have a cooperative, hard working team of employees, who have more than once demonstrated the ability to meet demands and challenges in a positive manner.

Recently you were called to a meeting at the corporate headquarters. Because of your effective leadership, the quality of the plant's production and the wealth of basic skills among the employees, a decision has been made to give your plant what it needs to upgrade the shop. However, if the workforce cannot effectively use the new equipment, the factory (and your job) will close, and the machinery will be moved to another facility.

All the new tools are computer driven; they are state-of-the-art Computer-Aided-Manufacturing (CAM) machines. In order to produce the product, the machines must be programmed and the instructional manuals are written at an eighth-grade level. As a way to anticipate and possibly head off problems in teaching CAM operations, you asked all employees to take a reading proficiency test. The idea of the test was met with suspicion and reluctance, but you explained that there are instructional manuals coming onto the work floor, and you need to determine what the appropriate level of writing for these books would be. This is not true, since the books are already written, but you feel that explaining the concept this way will lessen resistance. Either way, it is a test that will be perceived as a way to ascertain whether or not workers could "measure up" to the reading requirements of the documents.

The results of the test are shocking. One-fifth of the younger workers, about one hundred thirty-five people, were in fact reading below the sixth grade level. Of the older workers, almost one-half, about one hundred and fifty people, are at that level.

You need to establish and implement a remedial reading and comprehension program at once. As you see it, here are your problems:

1. *Time is critical. The machines will arrive and be set up within six weeks, and an upturn in production will be expected soon after that.*

2. *The employees may volunteer some time, but most or all of the class time will have to be on the clock. This is, of course, very expensive since you will be paying full wages to people who are in class and not on the production line.*

3. *You are worried that those who go to these classes will be seen as less intelligent than the rest. You want a way to present the need for these classes that is not insulting or demeaning, and that minimizes the opportunity for embarrassment.*

The employees cannot effectively use the new equipment without basic skills.

4. You want to figure out how long to work with those who have serious reading deficiencies, and if they are not trainable, how to terminate them. You are sure that if there are any who cannot learn to read well enough to succeed, they will be in the older, less educated group. You are worried that you may be facing age discrimination suits.

No wonder production is down! This manager has little or no faith in his or her employees and it must have shown up long before. Let's back up to the fact that there are two distinct populations of workers in this shop who do not interact. If they are not communicating socially, they are certainly not communicating on the production line. As a manager faced with such a situation, you should take proactive steps to bridge these gaps. Buddy systems, team management meetings that include representation from both groups and company-sponsored social gatherings would all be of help to break down these barriers.

In this situation, the creation of a site-management team should be considered mandatory. Explain to your team that production is down, and ask for their input to help solve the production problems. If you need to amend some of their ideas, explain why. Be open, honest and most of all, willing to change.

Do not try to deceive your workers about the nature of the manuals. Some clever soul will think to check the copyright date, and you will be forced to spend your time trying to back away from an unfortunate lie that will have destroyed your credibility in an already distrustful atmosphere.

When the CAM equipment arrives, call a meeting of the site management team in order to discuss how best to provide on-site training for the company. Give them the manuals and ask for guidance as to how the CAM system can be up and running in a minimum amount of time. If the manuals seem complicatd to them, they will probably suggest that you provide time for some staff development. Approaching the problem in this way will avoid making an issue of the reading abilities present in the employees. Find one of many competent educators who do on-site training in industrial settings and work with this person to develop some visual as well as hands-on learning guides. Give the entire group a pretest; part oral, part written and part hands-on, designed to assess their strengths and weaknesses in computer skills, not literacy. Those who pass the pretest with flying colors should be designated peer tutors to small groups of learners. The peer groups can meet on a rotating schedule so that most of the plant is functioning when one group is working.

In one week it should be clear who will pick up the skills quickly and who will not. If the number of those experiencing difficulty is small, meet with them individually to work the problem through. Tell them you have noticed that they seem to be experiencing some difficulty with the information and you are wondering how you can help. If they tell you they hate the whole thing and want out, that is their decision. Tell them sincerely that you will miss their contribution to the company and facilitate their leaving with letters of recommendation and other forms of support to help them find new jobs. If they tell you that they want to learn but the reading is difficult, ask them if some small group instruction in reading technical manuals would help. If they admit they cannot read, be ready to provide opportunities and/or community resources that can help them with this very real problem. Their talents and skills are too valuable to your company to dismiss them because of a learning disability.

The issues here are very sensitive and must be handled with great care. Not everyone learns by reading a manual. Many people learn through a hands-on approach of trial and error. Both learning styles are equally successful and valid. You must also realize that the pretest suggested in the scenario may be a skewed form of assessment. A test of basic reading skills will probably not be structured to measure what you need to know. If a manager had a sick employee, he or she would not call on a muffler repair person to treat the worker. Managers who want employees to learn to run a machine should not let the people who write manuals determine who will or will not experience success in this task. It is an educational issue, and should be handled by you working with educators and peer tutors.

OF FIGHTS AND FENCE LINES

Your factory's parking lot is fenced in. Several yards outside the fence is a railroad spur which leads into the factory. The company's property line is just beyond the spur. Yesterday an argument began between two men on the plant floor. After work they drove out of the parking lot, over the spur and off company property. They then jumped out of their cars and started fighting. Everyone in that part of the parking lot could see what was going on, and after a while some ran over to break it up. Neither man was badly hurt.

The next morning you learn from one of the supervisors that the fighters are still angry and that it may happen again after work today. You don't want that to happen, but are not sure how to stop it. After all, they were careful to get off company property before fighting, and so were not in violation of a policy that could have called for their firing. However, you are concerned that they might be hurt if this happens again. Two concerns of greater scope are the effects their continued hostility will have on the workplace, even if it is only verbal, and the possibility of others becoming involved. Finally, it occurs to you that some employees might think of the area outside the property line as a spot for settling disputes, with others watching through the fence. This is a tradition you do not want to see get started.

What can you do right away before the shift ends? What can you say or do about the potential for similar incidents?

The fighters are still angry and they may fight again.

Although this seems like a potential monster of a problem that could increase in size and consume everyone in a fervent desire to run across the railroad tracks and fight at the drop of a hat, this manager needs to take a breath and realize that this has never happened before. It is an isolated incident and should be treated as such. Remember when we discussed serious disruption earlier in this book, we said that a manager should be able to show a pattern of disruption before creating rules that limit behaviors. There simply is no pattern here. And what would the rule be? No fighting within sight of the factory? No fighting within fifteen minutes of getting out of work? The company's property lines are clearly defined and cannot be extended. For instance, will this manager ban fights that occur just off the property line? What then will be the response to two employees who engage in a brawl at 2 A.M. on a Sunday morning in the front yard of a third employee who witnesses the fight? Clearly it is not the time or place of the argument that is the main issue in this scenario, but rather it is the manner in which every employee chooses to resolve conflicts with which the manager should be concerned.

The first piece of good news here is that the employees did drive off company property to fight. They are clearly demonstrating a respect for company rules and for management by this action. As a manager moves to work through this problem, it must be kept in mind that the fact that these two employees understand and respect company rules is no small issue. When the manager begins to sort this out, both employees should be invited into the office at the same time. The manager is on a peacekeeping mission and needs to have both parties represented. Talking to one at a time may only increase suspicion and anger.

As the manager begins to talk with these employees, it is most important that a clear focus be kept on what role each is fulfilling as they work together to find a reasonable resolution to whatever the problem might be. The manager is not the parent and these workers are not errant children. The issue is one of company harmony and productivity. The manager should approach this meeting as a genuine inquiry to explore with the two workers how the conflict between them can be resolved in favor of the greater welfare. Express genuine interest in mutually discovering ways that the issue can be put to rest. Let them know that you are available and willing to assist in any way that might be appropriate, but keep in mind that you don't own this problem, they do. Be careful to keep those lines from blurring. If in the course of your discussion you learn that a policy you have created contributed to their hostility, be prepared to assume whatever portion of ownership is appropriate and promise to fix that piece of the problem.

Using strategies from William Glasser's *Reality Therapy*, ask the workers what each will do to resolve the conflict and avoid any further hostile actions. Get a commitment from each and thank them again for respecting the company enough to have taken their fight over the property line even though they must have both been very angry at the time. Let them know that you are on their side, that you value their contributions to the company and that your door is open for further consultation should they feel that it is appropriate. In other words, you will be happy to talk again with both of them if they feel that it will help. You can also let them know that if one of them has a personal issue that is contributing to the stress, you will be happy to meet on a one-to-one basis.

Now for the bigger picture. As manager, you need to ask yourself if you provided any on-site training in strategies for peaceful conflict resolution. A brief one- or two-hour session that provides workers with some specific techniques for calmly resolving problems with each other as well as with you might be a very good idea. Another idea that is catching on is peer mediation. Train all workers to be peer mediators, mediators who can listen objectively to both sides of an issue and help fellow workers find solutions to interpersonal problems that are mutually beneficial. Let new employees know that this is the system for solving problems in your shop, and provide them with a training session as part of their orientation.

You really don't have a big problem, but it might become one if you begin making a lot of rules or conversely adopt a "boys will be boys" approach.

Fighting is disruptive and dangerous but lectures and punishment will not stop it. What your employees need are some alternative strategies for airing grievances and resolving problems. These strategies can also translate into helping workers create more peaceful home environments.

THE INTERNAL ASSASSIN

Six months ago, you and Sandy were being considered for a promotion to supervisor of your department. You have both filled in from time to time as temporary supervisors in the absence of the regular staff. You are about the same age, with comparable education and experience. Management did not have any significant differences upon which to base a decision as to who would be awarded the new title. To your pleasure, they chose you.

Soon after you assumed your new duties, Sandy started to become quieter, grumpier and slightly difficult to work with. You knew that Sandy was having some financial and personal problems, so you felt it better to ignore the behavior and just act in a supportive manner. However, despite being pleasant and polite, your efforts at friendship and offers of "help with any problem" have been ignored.

Now, six months after your promotion, you have a supervisory problem that you may have waited too long to address. Since you are a new manager, you feel that your performance is being closely watched, and it is becoming obvious that something must be done.

Sandy is a constant gossip but does an acceptable job, just nothing extra. Sandy finds fault with everyone else and in general is a crabby disrupter of attitudes, a source of half-truths and inflammatory information.

You have decided that it is time for a face-to-face discussion. However, thinking about what to do, several questions have occurred.

A constant gossip.

1. *Since you are former co-workers, and in the past have shared a drink or three after work, should the discussion be over lunch or dinner, rather than in your office? Is that a bad idea because it is too friendly a setting to deal with corrective action? Is it a good idea because it allows for a comfortable, non-threatening setting which may reawaken some of the companionship feelings that were there before the change?*

2. *What do you say? What do you ask for? The problem is not slumping sales or low production, where you could set measurable standards. What if Sandy says "I don't know what you are talking about." You are afraid this could degenerate into a "No I didn't. . . . Yes you did" finger pointing match.*

3. *If there is a marked improvement in performance, do you comment? What do you say? How do you sound sincere and not condescending?*

4. *If there is a slight improvement, do you act encouraging or disappointed in your next meeting, or a combination? What should you be sure to say? What should you never say?*

5. *How long do you wait, and how many discussions do you have, before you decide that it is best for you to fire*

Sandy? Assuming the worst, what documentation and records of your meetings and counseling should you have on file if there is a lawsuit?

This is a very difficult situation that will challenge all of your "people skills," patience and tolerance. You may not ever resolve it as well as you wish, but it is vitally important to remember that the way you handle your problems with Sandy will send a powerful message to all your other employees as to the depth of your character and your commitment to the success of each employee. Keep in mind that they are all witness to Sandy's moodiness and you would be naive to think that Sandy is not sharing disgruntled feelings with anyone who will listen. Employees may enjoy watching Sandy send your blood pressure soaring, after all the water fountain set often finds such encounters to have the same entertainment value as the Saturday Night Fights. Don't forget that you have been promoted over each and every one of them, not just Sandy. So first and foremost in your mind should be the phrase "Keep your cool." No matter what, keep calm, stay loose.

There is nothing more detrimental to a cooperative work environment than an internal assassin. If you put off speaking with Sandy because you are uneasy about what to say, you may have allowed all sorts of miserable feelings a chance to take root. This situation calls for a proactive approach. Meet with Sandy as soon as possible after the promotion has been announced. For any number of very good reasons, the meeting should occur in your office. Your relationship has changed. You can still be friends but now is not the time for a mixed message. You have become Sandy's superior and you need to begin building that relationship. If you and Sandy are not of the same gender, meeting in your office with the door ajar is even more important. The last thing you need to deal with are insinuations of sexual harassment or worse.

Sit at a circular table or in two facing chairs. Do not place yourself on the other side of the desk. If a desk seems as if it might serve as a needed security blanket, try holding onto a pencil instead. You are mending fences while at the same time establishing a new working relationship. So meet in a professional setting but retain a personal touch.

This is the time for honesty expressed in a judicious manner. Let Sandy know that if the situation were reversed you might be feeling resentment and disappointment. Go on to say that you value the relationship you both have worked to establish and it's important to you that it continue. Let Sandy know that you are looking for some help and support in a situation that is very new for you. Admit that you may make mistakes and will value any assistance and insight Sandy might have for you. Keep in mind that there were no significant differences between you to help management choose you for this position. Sandy has good information and can be a great help to you, but you will need to set that process in motion.

Do not offer to help Sandy with any problems. This can only come off as sounding condescending. Your personal goal for this meeting should be to keep an image in your mind of you sitting in Sandy's seat and Sandy sitting in yours. Say everything to Sandy that you wish would be said to you under the same circumstances.

Although the initial meeting should be in your office, if the relationship improves and you are able to reestablish your friendship, you might consider moving outside the office for a business lunch, especially if that was a pattern you had previously established. A drink after work is not a good idea. A shared drink during happy hour can often lead to sharing confidences. If Sandy is acting friendly but secretly still harbors a grudge, you may say something that will only come back to haunt you later. Be friendly but keep the friendship at arm's length.

If during lunch Sandy begins to probe for information that you should not be sharing, side step the questions with something like "I really want to talk about anything but work." You don't need to prove you are still Sandy's buddy by offering up juicy office gossip that could easily be traced back to you. As with any relationship, changes take time. Be patient but don't lose sight of the direction in which you want this friendship to head.

You hope things between you and Sandy will work out for the best. But if they don't, be prepared to follow through on correcting the situation. Even if you have moved in a proactive way to circumvent tensions, Sandy might still be the sort of person who is only happy when there is disruption going on. If you hold your meeting with Sandy and the grousing continues, you are probably dealing with someone who is out to sink your ship.

Be assured that slumping sales or low production do not need to be evidenced for you to be taking action. Your professional judgment of attitudes that do or do not support a productive work environment is all that is necessary for you to begin to take further steps. In this situation your best move is to begin by reflecting on what you have seen happening. This is the perfect opportunity to work on your I-Message skills. "I've noticed that when I pass you in the hall, you look away and don't speak. I'm wondering if there is a problem we need to work on together." Phrasing the message in such a way removes the concept of blame. You are not pointing a finger but examining a situation you might be able to work on together. If Sandy's response is to shrug and act mystified, you can go on to say "In the past, we have usually spoken to each other during the day. What I am seeing is a different response lately. I just wanted to talk with you about it because I was concerned that there might be a problem."

Avoid saying you did this or you are not doing that. It is your perspective you are sharing. Sandy may or may not choose to acknowledge that there is a conflict. You can end the conversation at this point by saying that if Sandy does have some concerns, you are always available for a conversation. At least you will have conveyed the message that you care and want to have a smooth working relationship.

Any manager, old or new, who wants to build and sustain a solid working relationship with employees is always going to look for opportunities to give positive feedback. Employees want to hear that they are doing good work and compliments are always welcome. So your positive comments to Sandy should be part of a pattern of encouragement that you practice with all the workers. As such, it should not be interpreted as a condescension. If it is, then the problems are even more deeply rooted than you have previously realized.

Improvement is improvement. Even slight improvement should be noted and encouraged. Remain aware that your definition of a slight improvement may be worlds apart from Sandy's. If Sandy is making the effort to improve but you feel it is not enough, make sure your expectations are clear. If you hedged on your objectives in the previous meeting so as not to seem overbearing, you may have conveyed the message that you don't expect much. But go slowly. Sandy has improved and that's what counts. The message you should get from the improvement is one of support.

Now let's say that you have had your meeting with Sandy and expressed your concerns but nothing gets better. Sandy's behavior is effecting the productivity of other workers and no amount of I-Message consultations seem to help. At this point, it is time to move on to specifically addressing your concerns. You are the one who has been promoted and you should now begin to act decisively in the role of supervisor.

Before you meet, sit down and review, on paper if necessary, exactly what your concerns are and what you hope the outcome of the meeting will be. Work hard to keep the meeting focused on these issues so that you are not led into a mire of accusations that might come from Sandy. If Sandy accuses you of being unfair or condescending, a judicious response is "I'm sorry if I have done anything to offend you. I really want to work this out." It will cost you nothing to apologize, even if you are not sure what the apology is for. It will almost certainly catch Sandy off guard and will help to avoid a power struggle. Your ego is not as important as the relationship you are trying to repair. Rise above the situation, apologize and move on.

Most important, do not say "I'm sorry if I offended you, but . . ." The use of the work "but" indicates that you are not sincere in your apology. It sends a mixed message and it will cause Sandy to distrust you even more.

After your apology, begin as if with a new thought by saying something like, "We have spoken before about the tensions I sensed between us. I still see the same problems occurring. It is important for us to have a comfortable working environment that will be a place we enjoy coming to. I want us to work together on some specific ideas that will help us through this situation." Again, you are talking in general terms rather than pointing a finger at Sandy.

The goal you seek is one of mutual benefit. Keeping your eye on that goal will help prevent this meeting from degenerating into a petty exchange of accusations.

Review the reasons for this meeting and your expectations for future working relations. There is no reason to be stern. Your authority flows from your position, so your demeanor can be gentle and encouraging. If Sandy is unresponsive, ask "Is there anything you would like to say to me?" If you ask the question, be willing to hear the answer without getting defensive. However, if Sandy still refuses to communicate, end the meeting with a review of the major points that were covered and express thanks for the time you have spent together.

You always hope that termination won't be the final step, but if it is your moves are then determined by the best way to ensure Sandy is afforded full due process while protecting your workplace environment from undue disruption. The next meeting with Sandy should occur after you have developed a written plan of assistance for improvement. The plan should begin with a statement of the reasons why you feel it is necessary to take such a step followed by clear guidelines setting out your plan to remediate Sandy's problems. This can include counseling, retraining, staff development or whatever positive moves you feel will be most useful to Sandy.

The next portion of the plan should list your expectations for Sandy's behavior; for instance, the report that was due last week will be completed by a specific date, perhaps three days to a week in the future, etc. Although your posture is to help Sandy recover and turn the situation around, your plan of assistance for improvement should also act to begin "tightening down the screws." Clear expectations and deadlines are a legitimate part of the document you have drafted.

Discuss the plan with Sandy thoroughly. As you talk about it, avoid threats such as "If you don't do this we will..." Sandy is sure to understand the serious nature of the meeting because the expectations are so clearly defined and you will both sign this document. If Sandy becomes defensive and angry you can respond with statements such as "I know you're upset. I understand. I want to find a way for us to resolve these issues." Continue to avoid "I know you're upset, but . . ."

After you have both signed the plan of assistance, give Sandy a copy. Make sure Sandy knows how to contact the union representative, if one exists, and encourage seeking that person out to review the plan away from you. You have nothing to fear. You have acted to protect the legitimate workplace purpose of your company as well as Sandy's due process.

Your copy of the plan should go in Sandy's personnel file. Follow up on each of the items in the plan thoroughly. If the report has not been completed on the date set out in the plan, put a letter in Sandy's file stating as much. Create a detailed paper trail of the entire process. At this point, any meetings with Sandy to discuss aspects of the plan or expectations that have or have not been met should be documented on paper. Secret notes are not appropriate. Sandy should be kept well informed of and have an opportunity to review any papers being added to the personnel file.

If Sandy's attitude is not improving and the expectations of the plan of assistance are not being met, offer Sandy a transfer if that is an option. Such an offer should be stated in terms of wanting Sandy to explore options that might result in a more comfortable work situation elsewhere.

If you follow through on your part of the plan, offering assistance and support every step of the way, and Sandy does not, then you should shift to an adversarial posture. Write a formal letter to Sandy recounting the terms of the plan of assistance and your documentation of how those terms were not met. State that you will now begin procedures to move Sandy out of the company. You should again encourage Sandy to seek out the union representative so that full due process will be afforded this employee.

Many managers run from following through on the process involved in firing an employee. But if due process steps are taken, sincere efforts are made to assist the employee and a detailed paper trail is created, there is no need to be afraid of this process. You may be threatened with a lawsuit, but if your moves were based on your professional judgment, your Legitimate Workplace Purpose and your motives are free of any attempt to discriminate or deny employees their constitutional rights, you can feel a sense of confidence that you have worked through the problem in a manner that is legal and fair.

SOME FINAL THOUGHTS

THE REALITY CHECK

A new manager bursting with creative ideas can be the breath of fresh air employees long for. If you have the luxury of time, use it to get a feel for the workplace. Interview employees to determine what is successful in the job structure and what could use improvement. After significant input from your site-management team, other employees as well as upper-level management, develop a vision statement that reflects a consensus of opinion on what will define success in three years, five years and even ten years. Explain to your employees that you intend to use an even-handed and ethical approach to problem solving and conflict resolution. It will serve you well as you work to win the loyalty and respect of your workers.

However, the administrative structure above you may perceive your actions as those of a boatrocker. They may mistrust your innovative ideas as well as your motives. You must be aware that you are being closely watched as you step into the political fishbowl of a management position. Keep your administrator well informed of your every move. If that person seems uncomfortable with your ideas, be willing to take the role of a patient educator and explain your legal and ethical rationale for the decisions you and your site-management team are making. Provide your manager with a paper trail of the changes being instituted by your team and the reasons for those changes.

Be prepared for some resistance from the employees. They have been doing things in a certain way for a period of time and change can seem threatening. Work with them in small groups and in one-on-one situations to help them through the process. Most importantly, share with them the vision you and your team have developed. Make it the framework for all subsequent policy decisions. If employees understand where the changes are leading and what the new structure will look like, they will be much more willing to follow you.

Ambiguity destroys productivity. Well-thought-out and reasonable changes will help employees to flourish. Keeping the workers focused on the vision of where your plant or division is headed will clarify the need for change rather than create uncertainties.

Those employees who are opposed to the vision and remain so even after you have met and worked with them can choose to seek other employment options. As stated previously in the scenarios, give them your sincere support and offer them your help to identify other job opportunities.

In every thought, word and deed, reiterate that your primary goal is for the mutual success of all involved in the workplace environment. As you consistently model the behaviors that will help to bring your goal to a reality, you will see your workers following the pattern you set. Be at peace with your ego when you see that your plant is maintaining a level of high productivity with minimal input from you. Rejoice in the fact that you have set this smooth machine into motion and created the democratic, empowering atmosphere which you had planned.

CONCLUSION

The preceding scenarios have led you through a variety of situations that represent, for many managers, a murky swamp rife with alligators, quicksand and snakes. While none of the situations described are easy or fun to deal with, they need not mark the beginning of an ulcer nor the end of a career. A constitutional framework, solid ethical standards, proven counseling strategies and a creative imagination will serve you well as you respond in a proactive fashion to the trials and tribulations of maintaining workplace relationships and productivity.

None of the scenarios presented represents a formula for becoming a person who can solve any problem no matter what, but rather they should serve as springboards for developing inventive solutions to the wide variety of problems that arise daily in a typical workplace environment. Our goal has been to build your problem-solving skills by offering strategies that can provide you with a menu of options. When difficulties arise, get a firm grip on any legal issues that are involved and take the time to consider how you can resolve conflicts in ways that will leave dignity and working relationships intact. In summary, the law and ethics of any profession are at best fragile and difficult to manage when put into practice. Who is to know if legal concepts and professional ethics will be used to guide all actions and decisions? The choice is yours.

And now, let's revisit the scenario that began this book.

After nine years with Moneycrunch, Inc., you have risen to a middle management position. Moneycrunch is a firm providing financial analysis and investment services, with seventeen thousand employees in thirty-five U.S. cities, plus offices in Canada, England, Germany and France. For some time there have been rumors in circulation about cutbacks and layoffs, and recently they have begun to hit. The downsizing is partly due to some top management decisions, and in fact the CEO was recently fired. Additional problems are not the fault of anyone within the company, but rather the result of a long slow recession coupled with significant changes in the way the world's economic institutions work.

After a series of long, painful meetings and planning sessions, seven months ago you were forced to cut your staff from 60 to 45. At the same time, the company is aggressively seeking new clients, researching and developing new financial services and products, and paying extra attention to those clients who have stayed with the firm. Thus, although the staff has shrunk significantly, the work has not. In fact, in some areas it has increased. Now, seven months after the big layoff, you observe the following about your staff:

1. Morale couldn't be worse. Everyone is hunkered down, concentrating on their work. No one shares ideas or information. No one pitches in and helps anymore. As a result, an office that once worked well because of a great team effort, open flowing of concepts and news bulletins has become forty-five isolated workstations. In the past, people picked up phones for their co-workers when needed. They offered each other advice and freely shared it. They formed informal teams and pooled information and skills in a cooperative atmosphere. All this has almost disappeared.

2. *Most people are upset because they think that work from their fallen comrades has come more to their desks than others. There is a reluctance to complain, but you know this feeling is widely shared.*

3. *People are afraid that they will be laid off next. Some are already looking for other employment, cutting into their concentration and commitment to Moneycrunch. Although as a manager you know that no further cutbacks are planned at this time, you are not sure how to make them feel more secure. You are afraid you may lose some valuable people to new jobs at a time when you can least afford it.*

You know that the company's financial situation has stabilized. In fact, it is starting to turn upward, although new hires to ease the workload will not be brought onboard for several more months and then very slowly. It could be two years before your staff is up to 60 people again. Until such hiring does occur, how can you convince your staff that the worst is over? How do you begin restoring and rebuilding the team spirit that is almost gone? How do you get people to accept the new, heavier workload which appears to be long term, possibly permanent? How do you convince them the workload is shared as fairly as possible? How can you be most effective in this difficult situation? Top management is watching!

Okay. This is our last shot at it together. What's the glaring problem in the above scenario? That's right! Why should this manager assume he or she should even try to convince the staff that the worst is over. First of all, it clearly isn't. Until new staff can be hired the stress will not go down, but it can be changed into shared energy. Either way, the manager needs to identify the problems that can be fixed and those that cannot be. The only "fix" for the attitude problem is time and a shared focus. Trying to jolly workers into believing that "happy days are here again" is only going to result in their distrust when a second, even slight downturn, is experienced at any time in the future.

This is an excellent place to channel managerial energies with the understanding that you can only facilitate the process, you can't be the process. Restoring a sense of team

The only "fix" for the attitude problem is time and a shared focus.

spirit takes time, patience and understanding that it won't just happen. The most significant act a manager can perform is to consistently model the team approach. Top-down decision making, bringing one staffer or another into the office for a "how's it going chat," or instituting new policies that serve to protect one employee's job security to the detriment of others undermines the team and will lead to further fragmentation. Decisions need to be made openly and together. Workers should all know that they have equal input into the future direction of the company.

Remember: **"You don't get other people to do anything!"** These people know their jobs. It may well be that when the work got redivided some of it went to workstations staffed by people better able and trained to do other tasks. Let the workers examine what needs to be done, who is experiencing what overloads, and together decide if redistribution should occur. Most important, ask them if there are ways that some of the redirected work can be effectively shared among two or three people, if some of it can be condensed down, and if some tasks need to be let go because they represent more of a problem than a solution.

Top management is going to be very impressed. You have read this book, and you exude the confidence of a professional who is empowered through empowering workers. Congratulations!

BIBLIOGRAPHY

Gathercoal, Forrest; Judicious Discipline, Caddo Gap Press, 1991.

Gathercoal, Forrest; Judicious Leadership, Caddo Gap Press, 1991.

Gordon, Thomas; Teacher Effectiveness Training, McKay Publishing, 1978.

NOTES

NOTES

If you have enjoyed this book you will be pleased to learn that CRISP PUBLICATIONS specializes in creative instructional books for both individual and professional growth.

Call or write for our free catalog:

CRISP PUBLICATIONS, INC.
1200 Hamilton Court
Menlo Park, CA 94025

TEL. (800) 442-7477
FAX (415) 323-5800